THE 3RD GRADE SPELLING WORKBOOK

95+ GAMES AND PUZZLES TO IMPROVE SPELLING SKILLS

Ann Richmond Fisher

Illustrations by Joel and Ashley Selby

ROCKRIDGE PRESS

Copyright © 2022 by Rockridge Press, Oakland, California

No part of this publication may be reproduced, stored in a retrieval system, or transmitted in any form or by any means, electronic, mechanical, photocopying, recording, scanning, or otherwise, except as permitted under Sections 107 or 108 of the 1976 United States Copyright Act, without the prior written permission of the Publisher. Requests to the Publisher for permission should be addressed to the Permissions Department, Rockridge Press, 1955 Broadway, Suite 400, Oakland, CA 94612.

Limit of Liability/Disclaimer of Warranty: The Publisher and the author make no representations or warranties with respect to the accuracy or completeness of the contents of this work and specifically disclaim all warranties, including without limitation warranties of fitness for a particular purpose. No warranty may be created or extended by sales or promotional materials. The advice and strategies contained herein may not be suitable for every situation. This work is sold with the understanding that the Publisher is not engaged in rendering medical, legal, or other professional advice or services. If professional assistance is required, the services of a competent professional person should be sought. Neither the Publisher nor the author shall be liable for damages arising herefrom. The fact that an individual, organization, or website is referred to in this work as a citation and/or potential source of further information does not mean that the author or the Publisher endorses the information the individual, organization, or website may provide or recommendations they/it may make. Further, readers should be aware that websites listed in this work may have changed or disappeared between when this work was written and when it is read.

For general information on our other products and services or to obtain technical support, please contact our Customer Care Department within the United States at (866) 744-2665, or outside the United States at (510) 253-0500.

Rockridge Press publishes its books in a variety of electronic and print formats. Some content that appears in print may not be available in electronic books, and vice versa.

TRADEMARKS: Rockridge Press and the Rockridge Press logo are trademarks or registered trademarks of Callisto Media Inc. and/or its affiliates, in the United States and other countries, and may not be used without written permission. All other trademarks are the property of their respective owners. Rockridge Press is not associated with any product or vendor mentioned in this book.

Series Cover Designer: Patricia Fabricant
Series Interior Designer: Brian Lewis
Art Producer: Alyssa Williams
Editor: Sasha Henriques
Production Editor: Jael Fogle
Production Manager: Jose Olivera

Illustrations © Joel and Ashley Selby

Paperback ISBN: 978-1-63878-735-8
R0

CONTENTS

Introduction v

Animal Words 1

Sports Words 13

Art Words 25

Music Words 31

Map Words 37

City Words 49

Science Words 61

Technology Words 67

Measurement and Math Words 73

Earth Words 85

Space Words 91

Everyday Words 97

Extra Practice 110

Answer Key 118

INTRODUCTION

Welcome to *The 3rd Grade Spelling Workbook*! Specially designed for your third grader, this fun workbook will take them on a unique spelling adventure. Words are organized around topics third graders will find useful and fun—from unusual animals to things you find in outer space. They'll even begin to learn about synonyms!

The book is arranged in sections by theme and features 180 words to practice. Students are likely to encounter most of these words in the world around them and find them useful in other areas of learning. In each section, the first 10 words are a bit easier than the second set of words. There is also an extra section at the end that offers even more practice.

Students will practice the spelling and meanings of these words by completing lots of engaging puzzles. As a parent or teacher, you should be sure the student understands the directions for each activity. You should also discuss the meanings of any words that are new to your child.

I have had so much fun creating this book. As a former teacher, it combines my love of spelling and word games with my desire to create fresh, engaging content for learners and their families. It's been a dream project! I truly hope that that you and your student have as much fun with this book as I had making it. Now turn the page and dive right in!

Words to Learn: ANIMAL WORDS

Write each word in the blank.

1. bear   _____
2. lamb   _____
3. mouse   _____
4. skunk   _____
5. turtle   _____
6. snail   _____
7. wolf   _____
8. zebra   _____
9. panda   _____
10. hamster   _____

Write your hardest words again here:

_____

_____

PUZZLE 1

Bubbles!

Color in the bubbles you need to spell each word from the box. Unscramble the leftover bubbles to spell another word from the list on page 1. Write that word in the blank.

zebra   mouse   skunk   wolf   turtle   snail

New word: _____

PUZZLE 2

ABC Order

Circle the first letter of each word in the box. Write all eight words in ABC order in the blanks.

bear	lamb	hamster	mouse
zebra	skunk	panda	wolf

1. _____
2. _____
3. _____
4. _____
5. _____
6. _____
7. _____
8. _____

Write a sentence using the first animal on your list.

_____

_____

Words to Learn: Animal Words

PUZZLE 3

Box Stop

Write one word from the box in each blank space. You will not use all of the words.

| bear | zebra | lamb | mouse | skunk |
| wolf | snail | turtle | panda | hamster |

1. What two animals carry shells on their backs?

   _____   _____

2. What three animals are black and white?

   _____   _____   _____

3. What animal grows up to be a sheep?

   _____

4. What animal would you like to have as a pet?

   _____

Write a sentence with one of the words you have not used yet.

_____

_____

The 3rd Grade Spelling Workbook

PUZZLE 4

Word Search

Circle each word from the list that you find in the word search. Words may go up, down, across, or diagonally, both backward and forward. Write each word on the blank line as you find it.

V	T	U	R	T	L	E	S	S
R	E	T	S	M	A	H	I	N
P	S	S	Z	R	J	Y	C	X
W	L	N	E	W	Y	C	M	K
S	O	A	B	M	N	N	T	M
K	L	I	R	M	O	U	S	E
U	A	L	A	D	N	A	P	D
N	M	Y	E	X	F	Q	B	K
K	B	W	B	N	F	L	O	W

bear _____ wolf _____

zebra _____ snail _____

lamb _____ turtle _____

mouse _____ panda _____

skunk _____ hamster _____

Words to Learn: Animal Words

PUZZLE 5

Finish the Poem

Finish this rhyming poem. Use one of the spelling words from the box in each blank. (There are two extra words.) If time allows, draw a picture to go with your poem on another piece of paper.

| lamb | panda | snail | mouse |
| bear | hamster | skunk | |

When I fell from my bunk,

I landed on a ___ ___ ___ ___ ___.

When I dropped my pail,

It landed on a ___ ___ ___ ___ ___.

When I spilled my jam,

It landed on a ___ ___ ___ ___.

When I dropped my chair,

It landed on a ___ ___ ___ ___.

When I fell from the veranda,*

I landed on a ___ ___ ___ ___ ___.

When I fall asleep tonight,

I better hold on tight!

*A *veranda* is a large open porch.

The 3rd Grade Spelling Workbook

Words to Learn: MORE ANIMAL WORDS

Write each word in the blank.

1. goldfish _____
2. jellyfish _____
3. turkey _____
4. monkey _____
5. eagle _____
6. robin _____
7. giraffe _____
8. spider _____
9. grasshopper _____
10. octopus _____

Write your hardest words again here:

_____

_____

PUZZLE 6

Merry-Go-Round

Start at any letter and move around the circle, either forward or backward, to find one of your spelling words. Circle the first letter of the word you find. Write the word under each circle.

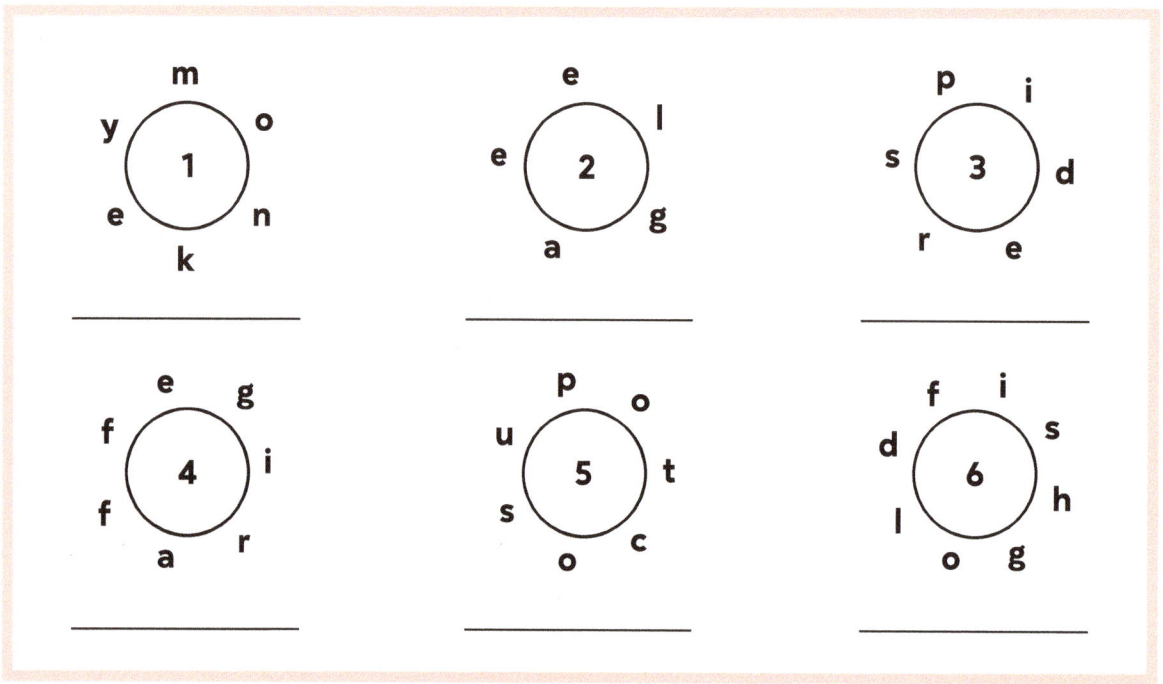

PUZZLE 7

Letter Sense

Fill in the missing letters to your spelling words so each sentence makes sense.

1. The o __ __ __ __ __ __ moved its eight arms around in the water.

2. A green g __ __ __ __ __ __ __ __ __ moved quickly across the field.

3. A j __ __ __ __ __ __ __ __ can swim freely in the water. It can also sting!

4. Outdoors I saw a large cobweb, spun by a s __ __ __ __ __.

5. A t __ __ __ __ __ is a large bird, often raised for food.

6. The r __ __ __ __ first appears in the spring. It lays light blue eggs.

7. Many families like to have a pet g __ __ __ f __ __ h.

Words to Learn: More Animal Words

PUZZLE 8

Crack the Code

Use the code to find your spelling words. Write each letter as you solve it.

1. @) 7 $ 3 9

   __ __ __ __ __ __

2. 1 5 2 4 & & 3

   __ __ __ __ __ __ __

3. 2) + 5 7

   __ __ __ __ __

4. 3 4 1 8 3

   __ __ __ __ __

5. 6 ? 2 $ 3 9

   __ __ __ __ __ __

6. 1) 8 ! & 5 # >

   __ __ __ __ __ __ __ __

1 = G	7 = N	$ = K
2 = R	8 = L	@ = M
3 = E	9 = Y	! = D
4 = A	+ = B	) = O
5 = I	# = S	& = F
6 = T	? = U	> = H

10   The 3rd Grade Spelling Workbook

PUZZLE 9

Places, Please!

Add each of your spelling words to this puzzle. Use the letters that are shown to help you. Cross off each word after you put it into the puzzle. Write each word again in the blank space.

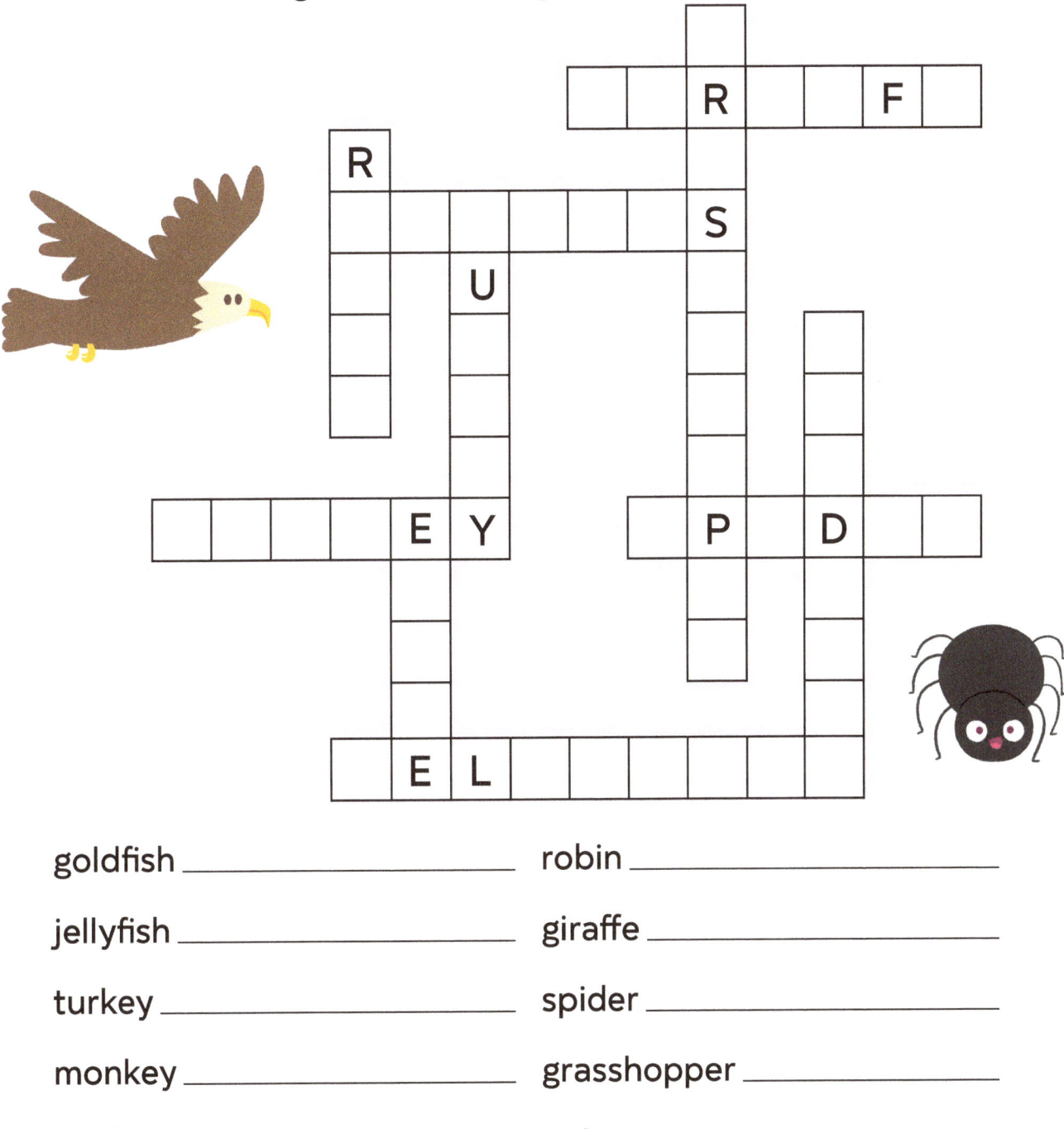

goldfish _____   robin _____

jellyfish _____   giraffe _____

turkey _____   spider _____

monkey _____   grasshopper _____

eagle _____   octopus _____

Words to Learn: More Animal Words   11

PUZZLE 10

Tic-Tac-Toe

Circle every word that is spelled correctly. Draw a line across three of them to score a tic-tac-toe. Write the misspelled words correctly in the blanks.

eagel	robin	jelyfish
turky	spider	girrafe
grasshoper	octopus	goldfish

_____

_____

Words to Learn: SPORTS WORDS

Write each word in the blank.

1. throw   _____
2. catch   _____
3. player   _____
4. coach   _____
5. teammates   _____
6. baseball   _____
7. football   _____
8. bowling   _____
9. swimming   _____
10. running   _____

Write your hardest words again here:

_____

_____

PUZZLE 11

Word Match

Write the letter for each spelling word from the box in front of the correct meaning. Write the spelling word in the blank at the end. If your work is right, you'll spell a fun word in the beginning blanks! Copy that word into the blanks at the bottom. An example is done for you.

1. __S__ Moving faster than walking __running__
2. ____ Person in charge of a team _____
3. ____ Person who takes part in a game _____
4. ____ Moving through water with arms and legs _____
5. ____ All who are on the same team _____

O. player

P. coach

R. swimming

S. running

T. teammates

Fun word: __S__ ___ ___ ___ ___

Write a sentence using a spelling word of your choice.

_____

_____

14   The 3rd Grade Spelling Workbook

PUZZLE 12

Word Search

Circle each word from the list that you find in the word search. Words may go up, down, across, or diagonally, both backward and forward. Write each word as you find it.

S	A	M	I	P	L	A	Y	E	R
W	W	E	T	S	R	R	O	R	L
G	N	I	L	W	O	B	A	E	L
A	R	F	M	C	A	T	C	H	A
S	E	T	A	M	M	A	E	T	B
J	O	H	Z	D	I	D	L	Z	T
T	E	G	N	I	N	N	U	R	O
C	O	A	C	H	E	M	G	K	O
T	H	R	O	W	A	R	U	R	F
O	L	L	A	B	E	S	A	B	K

running _____   teammates _____

swimming _____   coach _____

bowling _____   player _____

football _____   throw _____

baseball _____   catch _____

Words to Learn: Sports Words   15

PUZZLE 13

Be Choosy!

Choose the best answer to complete the sentence and circle it. Write the word in the blank.

1. It's fun to play sports with my _____.

   catch   teammates   running

2. On our team, we always listen to what our _____ tells us.

   player   football   coach

3. When Dad goes _____, sometimes he knocks down all the pins!

   bowling   running   swimming

4. In the summer, I like to go _____ in the lake.

   swimming   throw   running

5. I want to learn how to play the game of _____.

   teammates   swimming   baseball

6. How far can you _____ a football?

   throw   catch   coach

PUZZLE 14

Scrambles

Unscramble each set of letters and write the correct spelling words in the blanks.

1. o a c h c   _ _ _ _ _
2. n n n g u r i   _ _ _ _ _ _ _
3. t h a c c   _ _ _ _ _
4. m w i n s m g i   _ _ _ _ _ _ _ _
5. y r l a p e   _ _ _ _ _ _
6. b l o a t f o l   _ _ _ _ _ _ _ _
7. s t e m a m e a t   _ _ _ _ _ _ _ _ _

Words to Learn: Sports Words

PUZZLE 15

Crisscross

Choose two sports words from the box for each crisscross puzzle. (Use words that share the same letter.) Write the words in the puzzle. Write the words again on the lines below each puzzle.

| catch | coach | football | player |
| running | swimming | teammates | throw |

1.

[crisscross grid with C]

_____ _____

2.

[crisscross grid with O]

_____ _____

3.

[crisscross grid with N]

_____ _____

4.

[crisscross grid with A]

_____ _____

18   The 3rd Grade Spelling Workbook

Words to Learn: MORE SPORTS WORDS

Write each word in the blank.

1. skating _____
2. racing _____
3. biking _____
4. helmet _____
5. archery _____
6. arrow _____
7. soccer _____
8. golf _____
9. hockey _____
10. mascot _____

Write your hardest words again here:

_____

_____

PUZZLE 16

ABC Order

Circle the first letter of each word in the box. Write all seven words in ABC order in the blanks.

racing	biking	archery	soccer
golf	hockey	mascot	

1. _____
2. _____
3. _____
4. _____
5. _____
6. _____
7. _____

Write a sentence using the last word on your list.

_____

_____

PUZZLE 17

Merry-Go-Round

Start at any letter and move around the circle, either forward or backward, to find one of your spelling words. Circle the first letter of the word you find. Write the word under each circle.

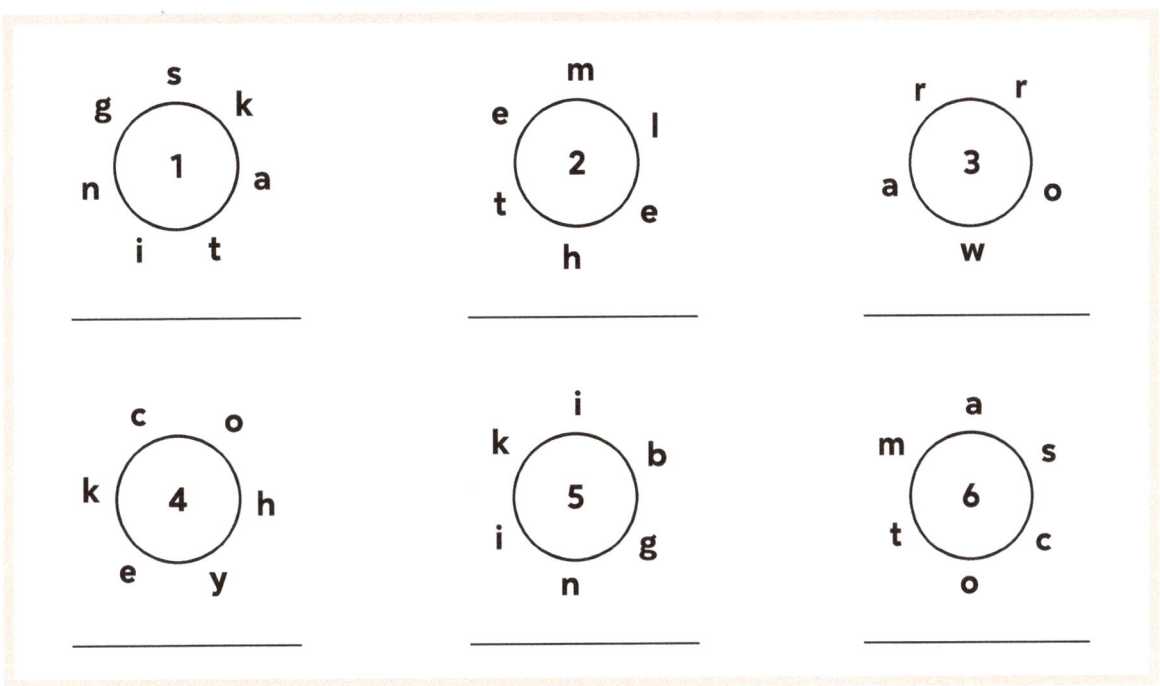

Words to Learn: More Sports Words   21

PUZZLE 18

Box Stop

Write one word from the box in each blank space. You will not use all of the words.

| skating | racing | biking | helmet | archery |
| arrow | soccer | golf | hockey | mascot |

1. Write the words that are made when –ing is added to each of these: skate, race, bike.

   _____ _____ _____

2. What should you always wear when riding a bike?

   _____

3. In archery, the archer uses a bow and an _____.

4. Players move around on ice skates to play the game of

   _____.

5. A game played around the world by kicking a black-and-white ball is called _____.

Write a sentence using your favorite sport word listed above.

_____

_____

The 3rd Grade Spelling Workbook

PUZZLE 19

Circle Time

In each line, circle the first, third, fifth, and seventh letters, and so on. Write the circled letters on the first blank. Write the leftover letters on the second blank. You will discover two sports words.

1. b h i e k l i m n e g t

   _____

   _____

2. a r r a c c h i e n r g y

   _____

   _____

3. s h o o c c k e e r y

   _____

   _____

4. s m k a a s t c i o n t g

   _____

   _____

Write a sentence using one pair of words listed above.

_____

_____

Words to Learn: More Sports Words

PUZZLE 20

Letter Sense

Add the missing letters to your spelling words so each sentence makes sense. (In one sentence, you will use the same word twice.)

1. If you like to be outdoors for a long time and do a lot of walking, then ___ ___ ___ f might be a good game for you.

2. The team's m ___ ___ ___ ___ t helped cheer them on to the winning goal.

3. Which do you like better, roller s ___ ___ t ___ ___ ___ or ice s ___ ___ t ___ ___ ___?

4. You must use a lot of arm strength in the sport of a ___ ___ ___ ___ r ___.

5. In the game of ___ ___ c c ___ ___, one player is always the goalkeeper.

6. It's fun to go ___ ___ k ___ ___ ___ with your family and friends.

7. When you go biking, be sure to always wear a h ___ ___ m ___ ___.

Words to Learn: ART WORDS

Write each word in the blank.

1. color _____
2. brush _____
3. crayon _____
4. chalk _____
5. drawing _____
6. picture _____
7. cartoon _____
8. print _____
9. weave _____
10. pottery _____

Write your hardest words again here:

_____

_____

PUZZLE 21

Bubbles!

Color in the bubbles you need to spell each word from the box. Unscramble the leftover bubbles to spell another word from the list on page 25. Write that word in the blank.

brush   crayon   cartoon   weave   picture

New word: _____

26   The 3rd Grade Spelling Workbook

PUZZLE 22

Tic-Tac-Toe

Circle every word that is spelled correctly. Draw a line across three of them to score a tic-tac-toe. Write the misspelled words correctly in the blanks.

coler	weave	potery
print	brush	drawing
cartune	crayen	picher

_____

_____

Words to Learn: Art Words

PUZZLE 23

Be Choosy!

Choose the best answer to complete the sentence and circle it. Write the word in the blank.

1. I like to _____ flowers, trees, and horses.

   chalk   color   drawing

2. Sarah painted a lovely _____ of a sunset.

   picture   weave   pottery

3. Will made a great piece of _____ from a lump of clay.

   brush   cartoon   pottery

4. We can use _____ to make a game on the sidewalk.

   print   chalk   weave

5. Grandma will _____ pieces of cloth together to make a rug.

   weave   brush   color

6. Be sure to clean your _____ when you are done painting.

   chalk   brush   pottery

PUZZLE 24

Word Search

Circle each word from the list that you find in the word search. Words may go up, down, across, or diagonally, both backward and forward. Write each word as you find it.

C	Q	T	Y	R	E	T	T	O	P
C	J	N	O	Y	A	R	C	P	I
A	N	P	E	V	A	E	W	R	M
R	B	W	I	N	E	N	M	I	J
T	V	R	T	C	D	Z	H	N	J
O	K	O	U	V	T	G	T	T	E
O	L	L	G	S	A	U	M	J	H
N	A	O	K	E	H	U	R	D	L
S	H	C	K	D	J	G	M	E	U
P	C	S	D	R	A	W	I	N	G

color _____   print _____

brush _____   picture _____

chalk _____   cartoon _____

crayon _____   pottery _____

drawing _____   weave _____

Words to Learn: Art Words

PUZZLE 25

Crisscross

Choose two art words from the box for each crisscross puzzle. (Use words that share the same letter.) Write the words in the puzzle. Write the words again on the lines below each puzzle.

brush   cartoon   chalk   color
crayon   drawing   picture weave

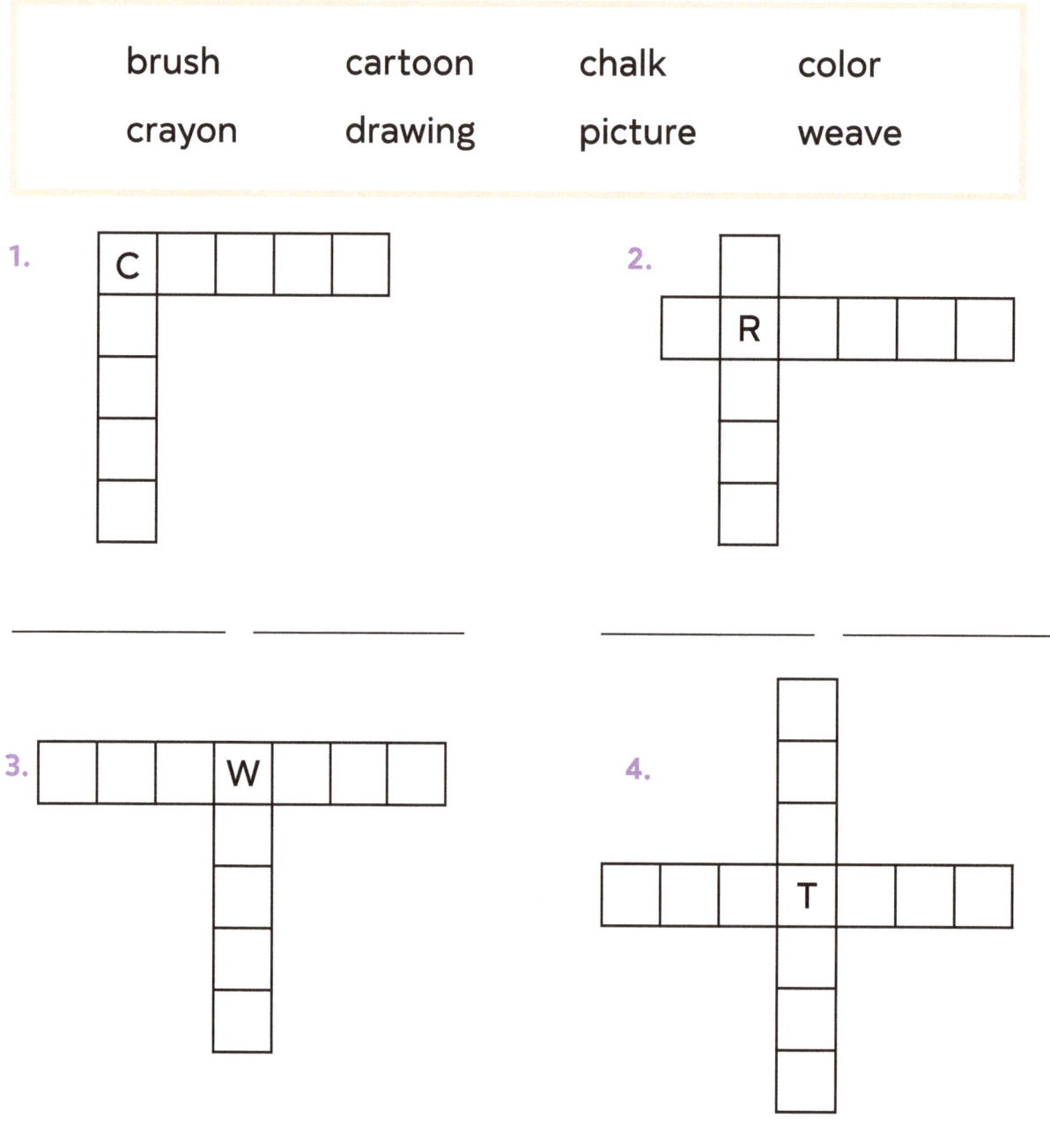

30   The 3rd Grade Spelling Workbook

Words to Learn: MUSIC WORDS

Write each word in the blank.

1. drums _____
2. trumpet _____
3. tuba _____
4. trombone _____
5. flute _____
6. fiddle _____
7. bagpipes _____
8. saxophone _____
9. banjo _____
10. piano _____

Write your hardest words again here:

_____

_____

PUZZLE 26

Merry-Go-Round

Start at any letter and move around the circle, either forward or backward, to find one of your spelling words. Circle the first letter of the word you find. Write the word under each circle.

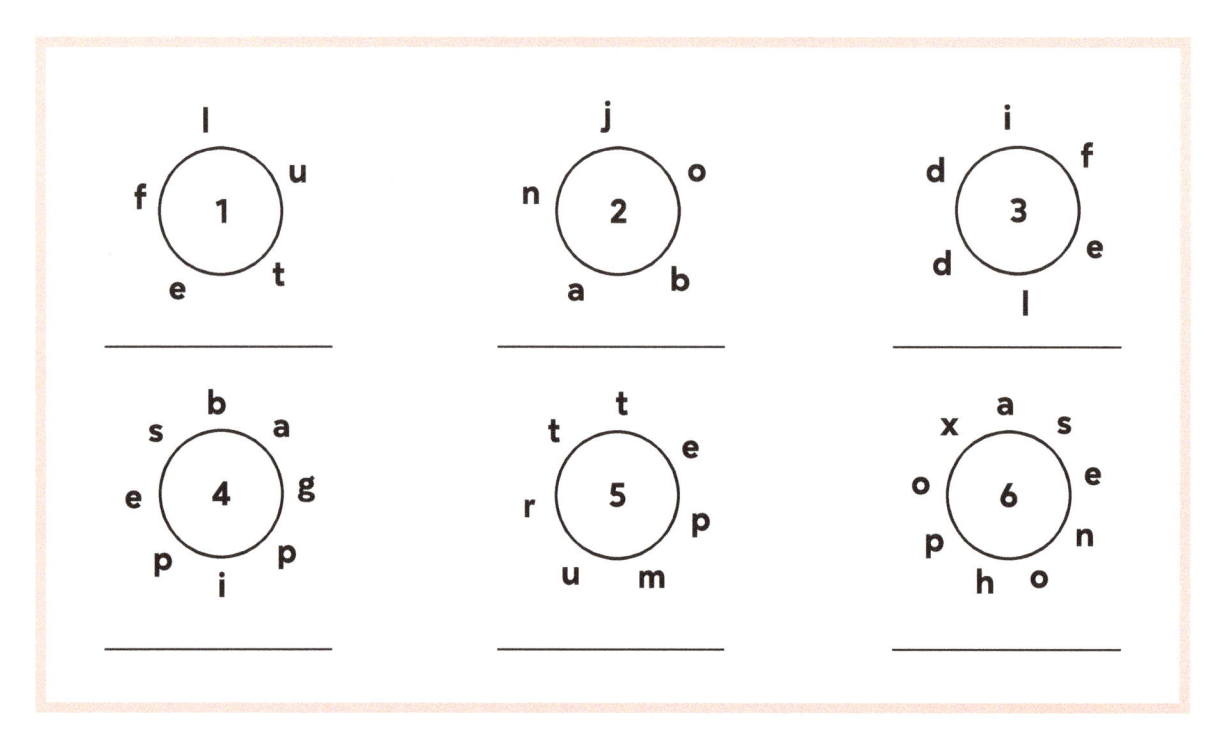

1. (circle with letters l, u, t, e, f) — useful

2. (circle with letters j, o, b, a, n) — banjo

3. (circle with letters i, f, e, l, d, d) — fiddle

4. (circle with letters b, a, g, p, i, p, e, s) — bagpipes

5. (circle with letters t, e, p, m, u, r, t) — trumpet

6. (circle with letters a, s, e, n, o, h, p, o, x) — saxophone

Write a sentence using the longest word from above.

_____

_____

_____

_____

32   The 3rd Grade Spelling Workbook

PUZZLE 27

Scrambles

Unscramble each set of letters and write the correct spelling words in the blanks.

1. b u a t   _____
2. a i o n p   _____
3. r s d m u   _____
4. p r u t t e m   _____
5. d e i f l d   _____
6. b o m r t o n e _____
7. n e x a s h o p o _____

Write a sentence using one of these spelling words.

_____

_____

Words to Learn: Music Words

PUZZLE 28

Places, Please!

Add each of your spelling words to this puzzle. Use the letters that are shown to help you. Cross off each word after you put it into the puzzle. Write each word again in the blank.

drums _____   fiddle _____

trumpet _____   bagpipes _____

tuba _____   saxophone _____

trombone _____   banjo _____

flute _____   piano _____

PUZZLE 29

Box Stop

Write one word from the box in each blank space. You will use some words more than once.

| flute | fiddle | bagpipes | piano | banjo |
| drums | trumpet | saxophone | tuba | trombone |

1. Which instruments are played by blowing into them?

   _____ _____ _____

   _____ _____ _____

2. Which horn has a long slide that the player stretches outward? _____

3. Which instruments can be played by using sticks or a bow? _____ _____

4. Which instruments make music by moving strings?

   _____ _____ _____

Write a sentence using any one of the spelling words.

_____

_____

Words to Learn: Music Words   35

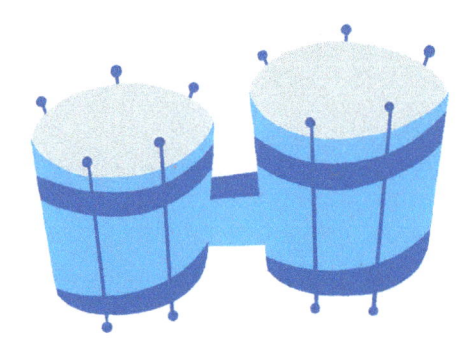

PUZZLE 30

Crack the Code

Use the code to find your spelling words. Write each letter as you solve it.

1. ♥ ✦ 7 6 5

    — — — — —

2. ★ 8 7 1 ☺

    — — — — —

3. 6 8 7 1 4 5 6

    — — — — — — —

4. 4 2 ✖ 3 △

    — — — — —

5. ♥ 2 ★ ★ ✦ 5

    — — — — — —

6. 6 8 △ 1 ? △ 3 5

    — — — — — — — —

7. ☺ ✖ 9 △ 4 # △ 3 5

    — — — — — — — — —

1 = M	7 = U	△ = O
2 = I	8 = R	? = B
3 = N	9 = X	★ = D
4 = P	☺ = S	✖ = A
5 = E	♥ = F	# = H
6 = T	✦ = L	

36 The 3rd Grade Spelling Workbook

Words to Learn: MAP WORDS

Write each word in the blank.

1. north _____
2. south _____
3. east _____
4. west _____
5. coast _____
6. gulf _____
7. river _____
8. stream _____
9. mountain _____
10. valley _____

Write your hardest words again here:

_____

_____

PUZZLE 31

ABC Order

Circle the first letter of each word in the box. Write all nine words in ABC order in the blanks.

north	south	east	west	coast
gulf	river	valley	mountain	

1. _____
2. _____
3. _____
4. _____
5. _____
6. _____
7. _____
8. _____
9. _____

Write a sentence using the second word on your list.

_____

_____

PUZZLE 32

Bubbles!

Color in the bubbles you need to spell each word from the box. Unscramble the leftover bubbles to spell another word from the list on page 37. Write that word in the blank.

north   south   east   gulf   valley   coast

New word: _____

PUZZLE 33

Word Search

Circle each word from the list that you find in the word search. Words may go up, down, across, or diagonally, both backward and forward. Write each word as you find it.

E	D	A	T	S	E	W	N	A
A	A	J	G	T	Y	N	O	G
M	Q	S	C	R	E	I	R	O
C	N	M	T	E	L	A	T	R
S	O	J	N	A	L	T	H	I
A	O	A	M	M	A	N	G	V
Z	S	U	S	Z	V	U	U	E
Z	R	J	T	T	G	O	L	R
P	K	W	Y	H	D	M	F	M

north _____ gulf _____

south _____ valley _____

east _____ mountain _____

west _____ river _____

coast _____ stream _____

PUZZLE 34

Be Choosy!

Choose the best answer to complete the sentence and circle it. Write the word in the blank.

1. We crossed the _____ by walking over a small wooden bridge.

   coast river south

2. The opposite direction of east is _____.

   north south west

3. A _____ is a part of the ocean that is mostly surrounded by land.

   gulf valley river

4. The part of the land that touches a body of water is called the _____.

   stream coast valley

5. It may be colder at the top of the _____.

   mountain west gulf

6. A grassy _____ runs between the two mountains.

   stream gulf valley

Words to Learn: Map Words

PUZZLE 35

Crisscross

Choose two map words from the box for each crisscross puzzle. (Use words that share the same letter.) Write the words in the puzzle. Write the words again on the lines below each puzzle.

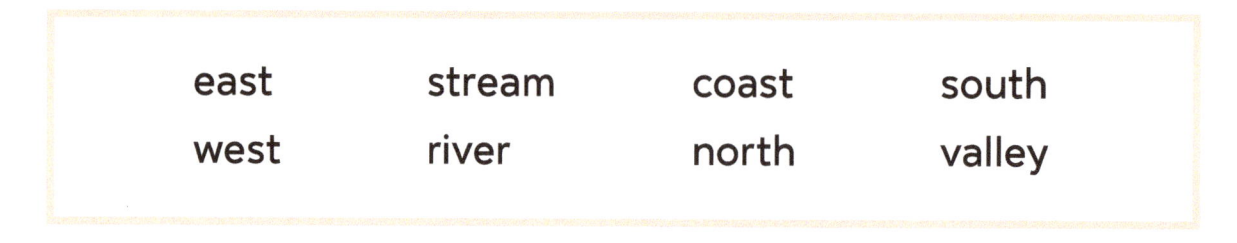

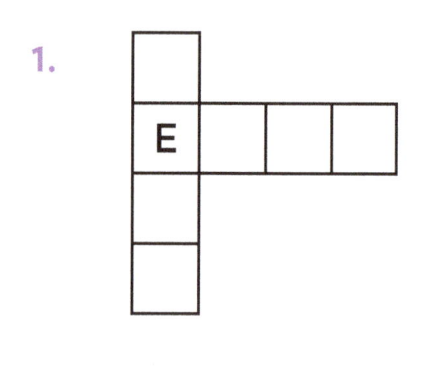

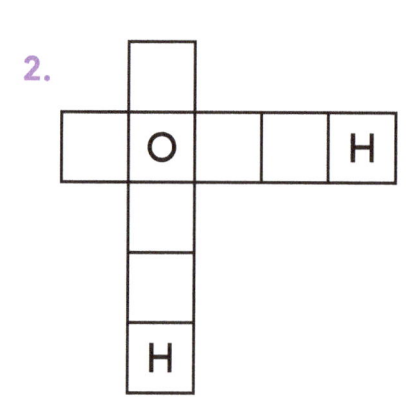

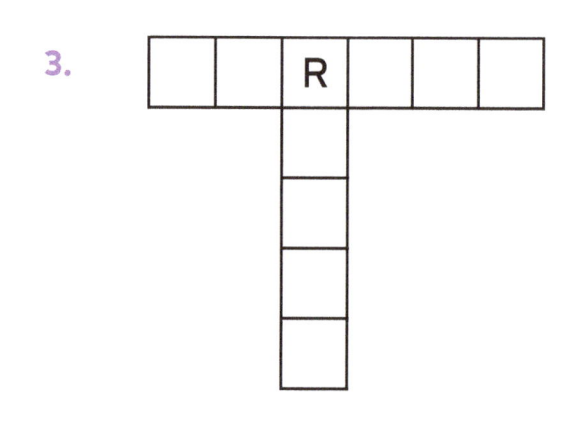

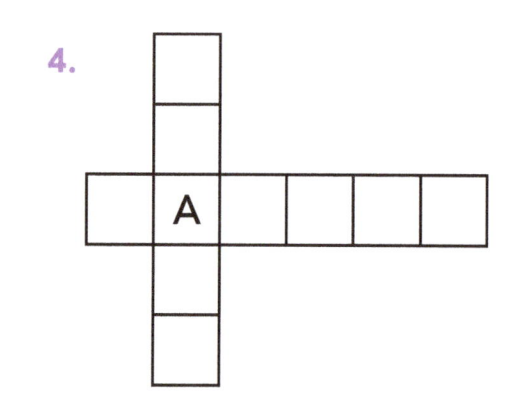

| east | stream | coast | south |
| west | river | north | valley |

1. E

_____ _____

2. O   H
    H

_____ _____

3. R

_____ _____

4. A

_____ _____

42   The 3rd Grade Spelling Workbook

Words to Learn: MORE MAP WORDS

Write each word in the blank.

1. cape _____
2. harbor _____
3. tundra _____
4. glacier _____
5. desert _____
6. border _____
7. nation _____
8. continent _____
9. world _____
10. globe _____

Write your hardest words again here:

_____

_____

PUZZLE 36

Merry-Go-Round

Start at any letter and move around the circle, either forward or backward, to find one of your spelling words. Circle the first letter of the word you find. Write the word under each circle.

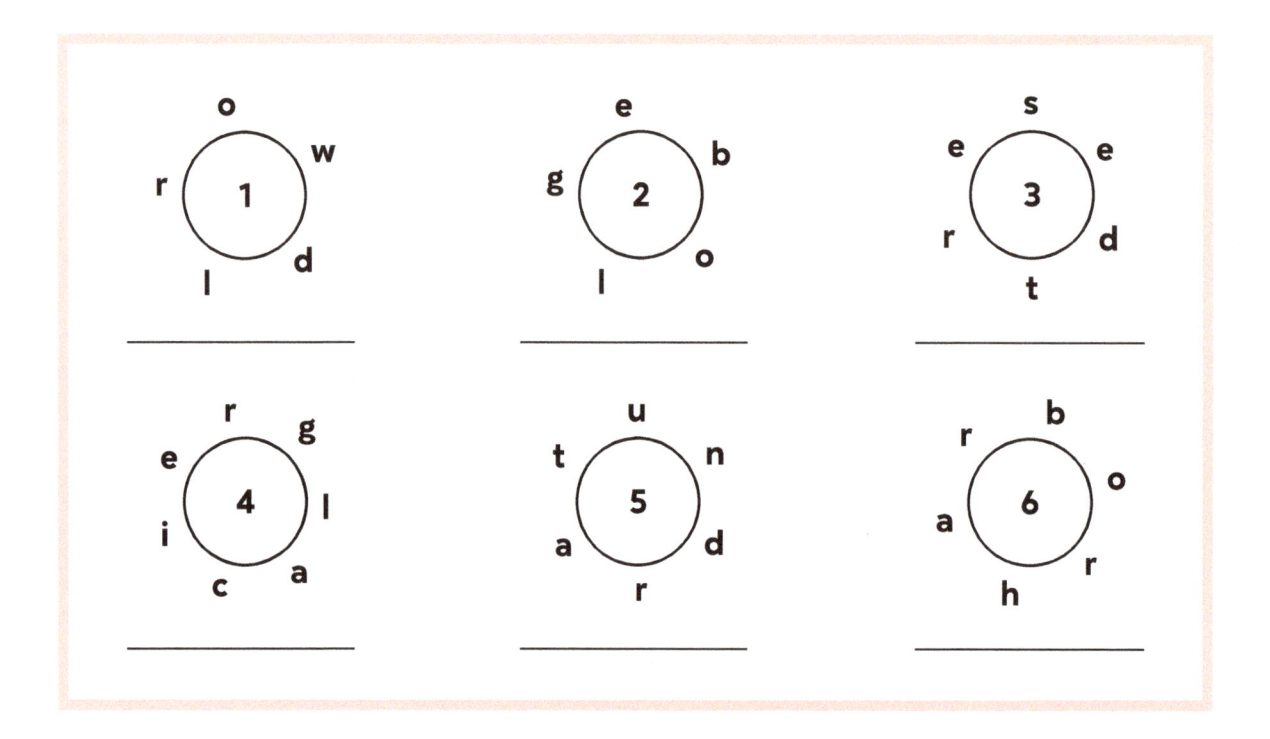

1. world
2. globe
3. desert
4. glacier
5. tundra
6. harbor

PUZZLE 37

Box Stop

Write one word from the box in each blank space. You will not use all of the words.

| cape | harbor | tundra | glacier | desert |
| border | nation | continent | world | globe |

1. Which object is a model of the world?

   _____

2. Which word describes a line between two countries?

   _____

3. Which word is a large mass of ice?

   _____

4. Which word has both of these meanings?

   a) A point of land extending into the sea

   b) A piece of clothing that ties around the neck

   _____

5. What is a treeless, flat area of land in arctic regions?

   _____

Words to Learn: More Map Words

PUZZLE 38

Circle Time

In each line, circle the first, third, fifth, and seventh letters, and so on. Write the circled letters on the first blank. Write the leftover letters on the second blank. You will discover two map words.

1. g w l o o r b l e d

   _____

   _____

2. n b a o t r i d o e n r

   _____

   _____

3. g t l u a n c d i r e a r

   _____

   _____

4. h d a e r s b e o r r t

   _____

   _____

Write a sentence using one pair of words listed above.

_____

_____

PUZZLE 39

Tic-Tac-Toe

Circle every word that is spelled correctly. Draw a line across three of them to score a tic-tac-toe. Write the misspelled words correctly in the blanks.

continet	dessert	tundra
glaceir	nation	bordor
cape	harber	world

_____

_____

Words to Learn: More Map Words

PUZZLE 40

Crack the Code

Use the code to find your spelling words. Write each letter as you solve it.

1. + 8 2 1 $ 2

   — — — — — —

2. ← 6 2 + 8 2

   — — — — — —

3. 1 $ 3 $ 2 ♦

   — — — — — —

4. △ 6 ♦ 5 8 △

   — — — — — —

5. ☺ 4 6 7 5 $ 2

   — — — — — — —

6. 7 8 △ ♦ 5 △ $ △ ♦

   — — — — — — — — —

1 = D	7 = C	♦ = T
2 = R	8 = O	★ = U
3 = S	+ = B	☺ = G
4 = L	$ = E	
5 = I	← = H	
6 = A	△ = N	

48   The 3rd Grade Spelling Workbook

Words to Learn: CITY WORDS

Write each word in the blank.

1. city _____
2. school _____
3. market _____
4. bakery _____
5. church _____
6. bookstore _____
7. airport _____
8. sidewalk _____
9. people _____
10. noise _____

Write your hardest words again here:

_____

_____

PUZZLE 41

Bubbles!

Color in the bubbles you need to spell each word in the box. Unscramble the leftover bubbles to spell another word from the list on page 49. Write that word in the blank.

| airport | church | noise | people | bakery |

New word: _____

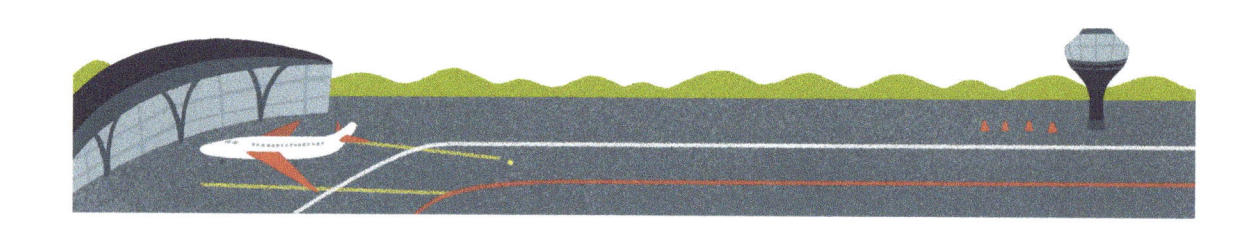

PUZZLE 42

Be Choosy!

Choose the best answer to complete the sentence and circle it. Write the word in the blank.

1. We took Grandma to the _____ so she could ride the airplane.

   church   airport   bookstore

2. There is always something good to eat at the _____.

   bakery   noise   sidewalk

3. Many, many people live in the _____.

   bookstore   school   city

4. During the parade, there was a lot of _____ from the crowds and the bands.

   market   noise   school

5. My dad likes to shop at the _____.

   school   people   bookstore

6. The market was full of _____ who were shopping for fresh food.

   people   noise   city

Words to Learn: City Words   51

PUZZLE 43

Word Search

Circle each word from the list that you find in the word search. Words may go up, down, across, or diagonally, both backward and forward. Write each word as you find it.

T	A	I	R	P	O	R	T	W	S
D	K	I	C	S	C	B	V	Z	S
M	L	C	I	T	Y	O	I	T	C
P	A	K	P	C	S	O	E	H	H
K	W	R	P	W	A	K	L	C	O
H	E	Q	K	N	K	S	P	R	O
J	D	J	Z	E	R	T	O	U	L
N	I	L	J	M	T	O	E	H	S
E	S	I	O	N	U	R	P	C	C
O	N	W	L	Y	R	E	K	A	B

city _____   bookstore _____

school _____   airport _____

market _____   sidewalk _____

bakery _____   people _____

church _____   noise _____

52   The 3rd Grade Spelling Workbook

PUZZLE 44

Word Match

Write the letter for each spelling word from the box in front of the correct meaning. Write the spelling word in the blank at the end. If your work is right, you'll spell a fun word in the beginning blanks! Copy that word into the blanks at the bottom.

1. ___ A large town _____
2. ___ A place to buy and sell goods _____
3. ___ A place where students learn _____
4. ___ A place where people worship _____
5. ___ A place where planes land _____

A. market
K. church
P. city
R. school
S. airport

Fun word: ___ ___ ___ ___ ___

Words to Learn: City Words

PUZZLE 45

Places, Please!

Add each of your spelling words to this puzzle. Use the letters that are shown to help you. Cross off each word after you put it into the puzzle. Write each word again in the blank.

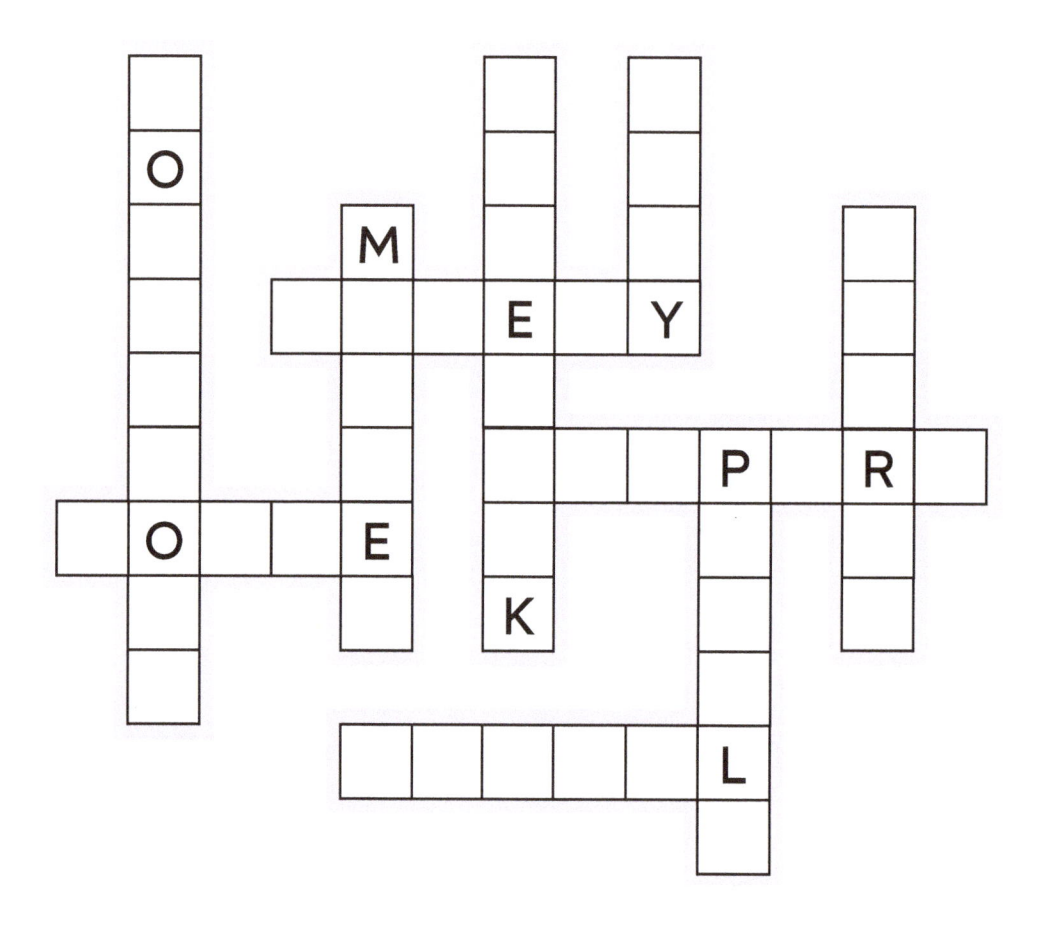

city _____   bookstore _____

school _____   airport _____

market _____   sidewalk _____

bakery _____   people _____

church _____   noise _____

Words to Learn: MORE CITY WORDS

Write each word in the blank.

1. taxi _____
2. subway _____
3. street _____
4. walking _____
5. shopping _____
6. hospital _____
7. offices _____
8. apartment _____
9. zoo _____
10. circus _____

Write your hardest words again here:

_____

_____

PUZZLE 46

Merry-Go-Round

Start at any letter and move around the circle, either forward or backward, to find one of your spelling words. Circle the first letter of the word you find. Write the word under each circle.

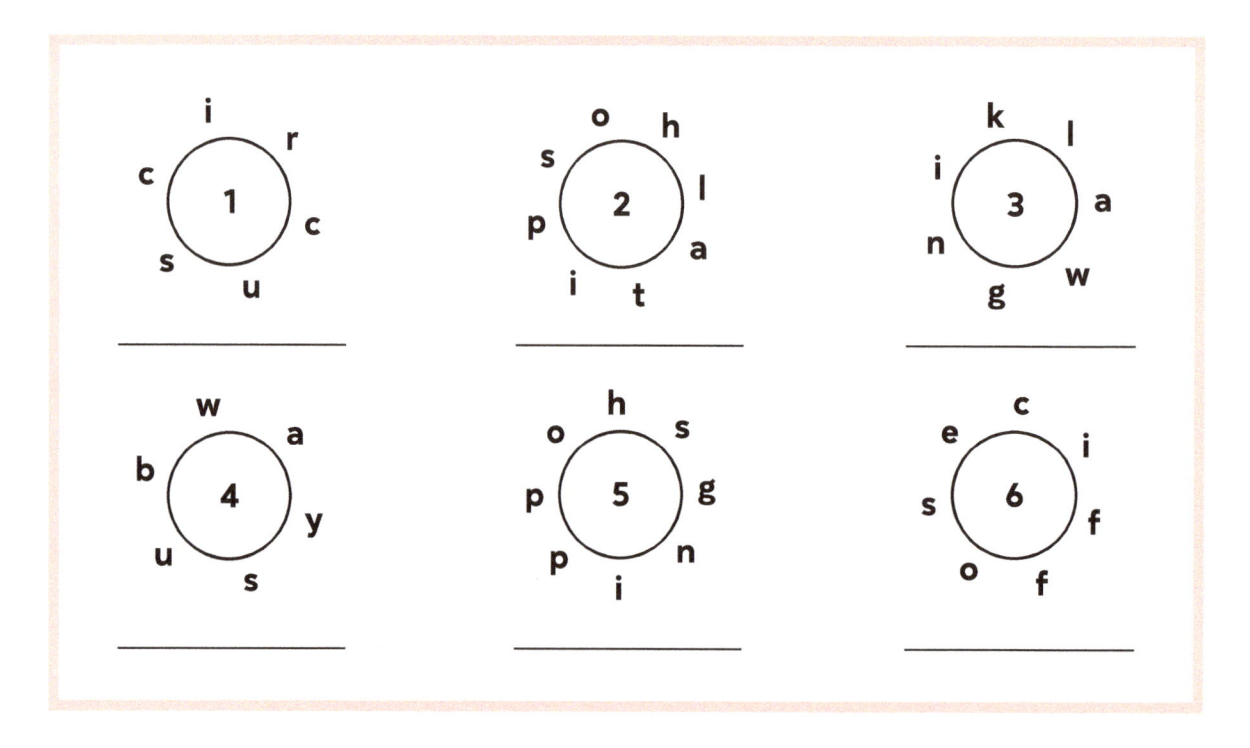

1. c, i, r, c, u, s → _____

2. s, o, h, l, a, t, i, p → _____

3. k, l, a, w, g, n, i → _____

4. w, a, y, s, u, b → _____

5. o, h, s, g, n, i, p, p → _____

6. e, c, i, f, f, o, s → _____

PUZZLE 47

Tic-Tac-Toe

Circle every word that is spelled correctly. Draw a line across three of them to score a tic-tac-toe. Write the misspelled words correctly in the blanks.

taxie	apartment	sircus
shoping	walkking	hosptal
street	offices	subway

_____

_____

Words to Learn: More City Words

PUZZLE 48

Box Stop

Write one word from the box in each blank space. You will not use all of the words.

| zoo | circus | offices | apartment | hospital |
| street | subway | taxi | shopping | walking |

1. Name three ways you can get around in the city.

   _____   _____   _____

2. Where might sick people go to get well?

   _____

3. In what building might many families live?

   _____

4. What are two fun places to visit?

   _____   _____

Write a sentence using any one of the spelling words.

_____

_____

PUZZLE 49

Circle Time

In each line, circle the first, third, fifth, and seventh letters, and so on. Write the circled letters on the first blank. Write the leftover letters on the second blank. You will discover two city words.

1. t z a o x o i

   _____

   _____

2. s s u t b r w e a e y t

   _____

   _____

3. w o a f l f k i i c n e g s

   _____

   _____

4. a h p o a s r p t i m t e a n l t

   _____

   _____

Write a sentence using one pair of words listed above.

_____

_____

Words to Learn: More City Words

PUZZLE 50

Letter Sense

Add the missing letters to your spelling words so each sentence makes sense.

1. We rode in a t ___ ___ ___ to go downtown.

2. We hoped that we would be in time to see the ___ ___ ___ c ___ ___!

3. Lots of people were ___ ___ ___ k ___ ___ ___ to get a good seat.

4. Families were watching from their ___ ___ a r ___ ___ ___ ___ ___ s.

5. Workers were watching from their ___ ___ f ___ ___ ___ ___.

6. The ___ t ___ ___ ___ ___ ___ ___ was full of animals!

7. It was almost like being at the ___ ___ o !

Words to Learn: SCIENCE WORDS

Write each word in the blank.

1. atom _____
2. matter _____
3. mass _____
4. compound _____
5. mixture _____
6. mineral _____
7. energy _____
8. light _____
9. rainbow _____
10. prism _____

Write your hardest words again here:

_____

_____

PUZZLE 51

Bubbles!

Color in the bubbles you need to spell each word in the box. Unscramble the leftover bubbles to spell another word from the list on page 61. Write that word in the blank.

| mineral | light | mixture | atom | prism |

New word: _____

Write a sentence using the words that describe what's happening in the illustration.

_____

_____

_____

62   The 3rd Grade Spelling Workbook

PUZZLE 52

Word Search

Circle each word from the list that you find in the word search. Words may go up, down, across, or diagonally, both backward and forward. Write each word as you find it.

C	M	I	X	T	U	R	E
W	O	B	N	I	A	R	R
N	K	M	P	Y	M	M	E
H	V	P	P	R	K	A	T
A	T	O	M	O	I	S	T
T	H	G	I	L	U	S	A
Y	G	R	E	N	E	N	M
L	A	R	E	N	I	M	D

atom _____   mineral _____

matter _____   energy _____

mass _____   light _____

compound _____   rainbow _____

mixture _____   prism _____

Write a sentence using one of these spelling words.

_____

_____

Words to Learn: Science Words   63

PUZZLE 53

Scrambles

Unscramble each set of letters and write the correct spelling words in the blanks.

1. o m a t   __ __ __ __
2. s a m s   __ __ __ __
3. t r e a m t   __ __ __ __ __ __
4. t h i g l   __ __ __ __ __
5. l i n e m a r   __ __ __ __ __ __ __
6. w r o n i b a   __ __ __ __ __ __ __
7. m i s r p   __ __ __ __ __
8. p o o n u d c m   __ __ __ __ __ __ __ __

Write a sentence using one of these spelling words.

_____

_____

PUZZLE 54

Crisscross

Choose two science words from the box for each crisscross puzzle. (Use words that share the same letter.) Write the words in the puzzle. Write the words again on the lines below each puzzle.

mineral	matter	atom	rainbow
mass	prism	mixture	energy

1.

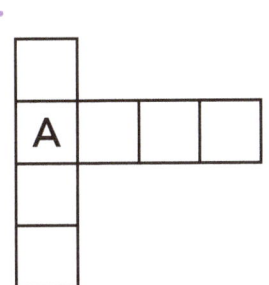

2.

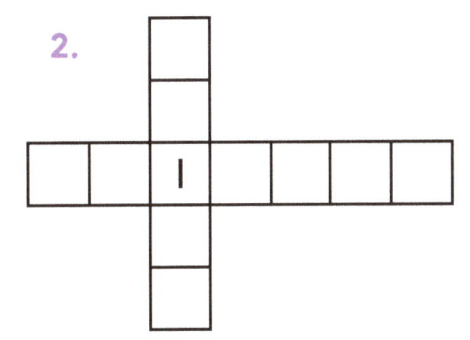

3.

4.

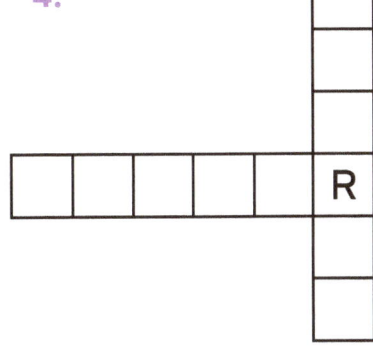

Words to Learn: Science Words   65

PUZZLE 55

Be Choosy!

Choose the best answer to complete the sentence and circle it. Write the word in the blank.

1. A _____ is a special solid object that breaks up rays of light.

   mass   prism   matter

2. When the light passes through the object in question 1, it is broken into the colors of the _____.

   rainbow   energy   mineral

3. We can combine salt and pepper in a _____, because the salt and pepper do not change when we combine them.

   mineral   matter   mixture

4. The smallest part of any kind of matter is an _____.

   energy   atom   light

5. If you have _____, you have the ability to do work.

   matter   mass   energy

6. The amount of matter in a body is its _____.

   mass   energy   mixture

The 3rd Grade Spelling Workbook

Words to Learn: TECHNOLOGY WORDS

Write each word in the blank.

1. internet　_____
2. tablet　_____
3. screen　_____
4. computer　_____
5. device　_____
6. password　_____
7. message　_____
8. cell phone　_____
9. camera　_____
10. robot　_____

Write your hardest words again here:

_____

_____

PUZZLE 56

Merry-Go-Round

Start at any letter and move around the circle, either forward or backward, to find one of your spelling words. Circle the first letter of the word you find. Write the word under each circle.

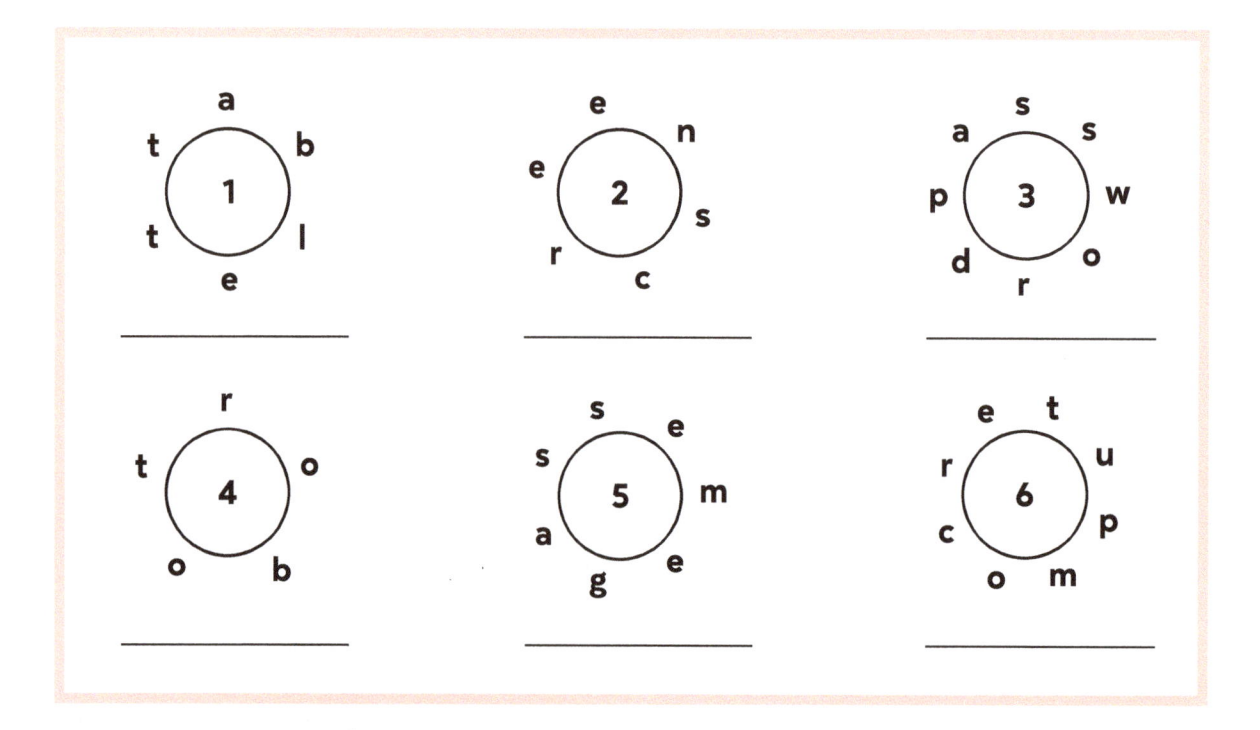

1. a, b, l, e, t, t → _____
2. e, n, s, c, r, e → _____
3. a, s, s, w, o, r, d, p → _____
4. r, o, b, o, t → _____
5. s, e, m, e, g, a → _____
6. e, t, u, p, m, o, c, r → _____

Write a sentence using a spelling word of your choice.

_____
_____
_____
_____
_____

PUZZLE 57

Word Match

Write the letter for each spelling word from the box in front of the correct meaning. Write the spelling word in the blank at the end. If your work is right, you'll spell a fun word in the beginning blanks! Copy that word into the blanks at the bottom.

1. ___ A huge, worldwide computer network _____

2. ___ A very thin, portable computer with a touch screen _____

3. ___ A secret set of letters and numbers that a user must supply before being able to use a computer _____

4. ___ A flat surface for displaying images on a TV or computer _____

5. ___ A text, post, or email sent from one person to another _____

A. tablet   M. password
E. screen   S. message
G. internet

Fun word: ___ ___ ___ ___ ___

Words to Learn: Technology Words   69

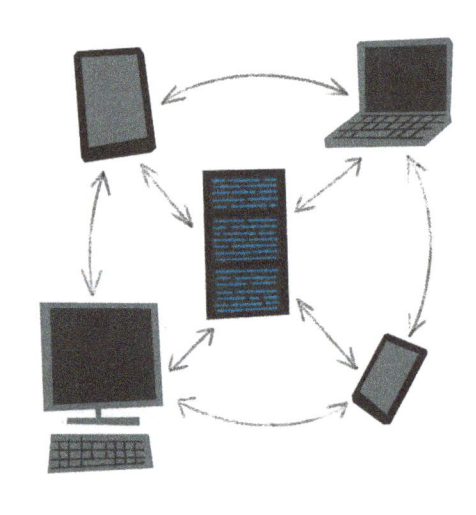

PUZZLE 58

Crack the Code

Use the code to find your spelling words. Write each letter as you solve it.

1. 3 6 ○ 6 4

   — — — — —

2. 1 ↑ 2 5 3 ↑

   — — — — — —

3. 4 ↑ ○ 7 5 4

   — — — — — —

4. ♦ 5 ↘ 9 1 5

   — — — — — —

5. 1 6 2 ★ 8 4 5 3

   — — — — — — — —

6. ☺ 1 3 5 5 ?

   — — — — — —

7. 9 ? 4 5 3 ? 5 4

   — — — — — — — — —

1 = C	7 = L	○ = B
2 = M	8 = U	? = N
3 = R	9 = I	♦ = D
4 = T	↑ = A	★ = P
5 = E	☺ = S	
6 = O	↘ = V	

The 3rd Grade Spelling Workbook

PUZZLE 59

Circle Time

In each line, circle the first, third, fifth, and seventh letters, and so on. Write the circled letters on the first blank. Write the leftover letters on the second blank. You will discover two technology words.

1. c r a o m b e o r t a

   _____

   _____

2. t d a e b v l i e c t e

   _____

   _____

3. c p o a m s p s u w t o e r r d

   _____

   _____

4. c i e n l t l e p r h n o e n t e

   _____

   _____

Write a sentence using one pair of words listed above.

_____

_____

Words to Learn: Technology Words

PUZZLE 60

Shape Shake-Up

Look closely at the letters in the shapes. Answer the questions below.

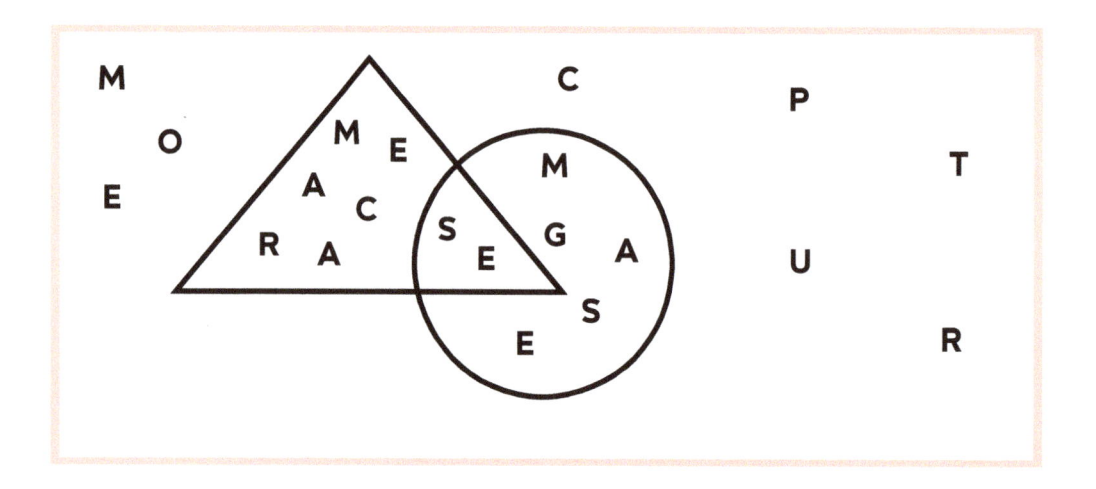

1. What spelling word can you make from the letters in the circle?
   _____

2. What spelling word can you make from the letters that are in the triangle but not the circle?
   _____

3. What spelling word can you make with the letters you haven't used yet?
   _____

Words to Learn: MEASUREMENT AND MATH WORDS

Write each word in the blank.

1. inch _____
2. foot _____
3. yard _____
4. mile _____
5. ounce _____
6. pound _____
7. weight _____
8. shape _____
9. circle _____
10. square _____

Write your hardest words again here:

_____

_____

PUZZLE 61

ABC Order

Circle the first letter of each word in the box. Write all nine words in ABC order in the blanks.

| inch | foot | yard | mile | ounce |
| pound | weight | circle | square | |

1. _____
2. _____
3. _____
4. _____
5. _____
6. _____
7. _____
8. _____
9. _____

Write a sentence using the fifth word on your list.

_____

_____

PUZZLE 62

Bubbles!

Color in the bubbles you need to spell each word in the box. Unscramble the leftover bubbles to spell another word from the list on page 73. Write that word in the blank.

foot   yard   ounce   weight   circle   square

New word: _____

Write a sentence using a spelling word of your choice.

_____
_____
_____

Words to Learn: Measurement and Math Words

PUZZLE 63

Box Stop

Write one word from the box in each blank space. You will not use all of the words.

| inch | foot | yard | mile | ounce |
| pound | weight | shape | circle | square |

1. Words that tell units of length are

   _____   _____

   _____   _____

2. There are 16 ounces in one _____.

3. An ounce is a unit of _____.

4. A triangle is an example of a _____.

5. Two more examples of this are

   _____   _____

Write a sentence using any one of the spelling words.

_____

_____

76   The 3rd Grade Spelling Workbook

PUZZLE 64

Places, Please!

Add each of your spelling words to this puzzle. Use the letters that are shown to help you. Cross off each word after you put it into the puzzle. Write each word again in the blank.

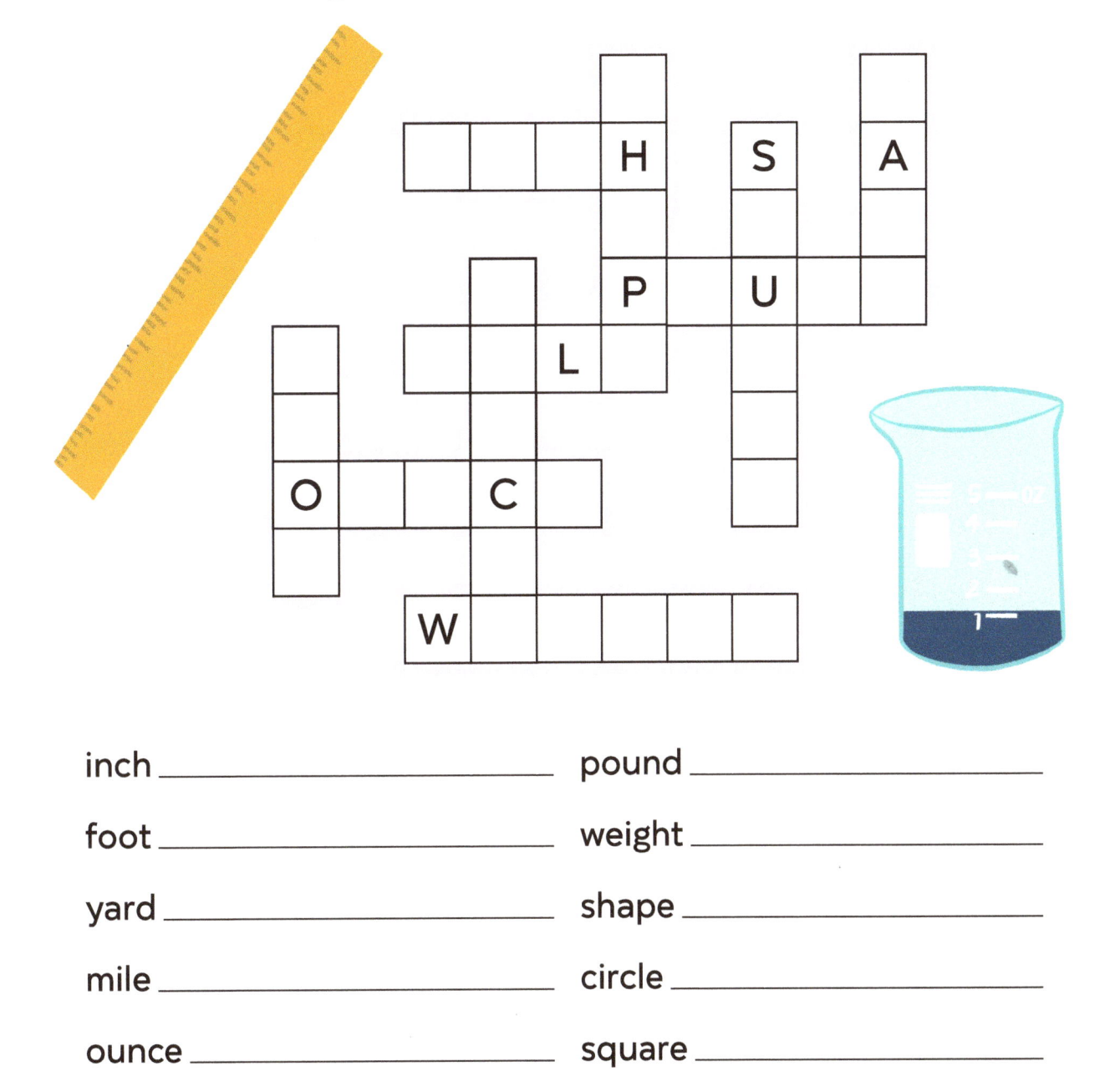

inch _____ pound _____

foot _____ weight _____

yard _____ shape _____

mile _____ circle _____

ounce _____ square _____

Words to Learn: Measurement and Math Words

PUZZLE 65

Shape Shake-Up

Look closely at the letters in the shapes. Answer the questions below.

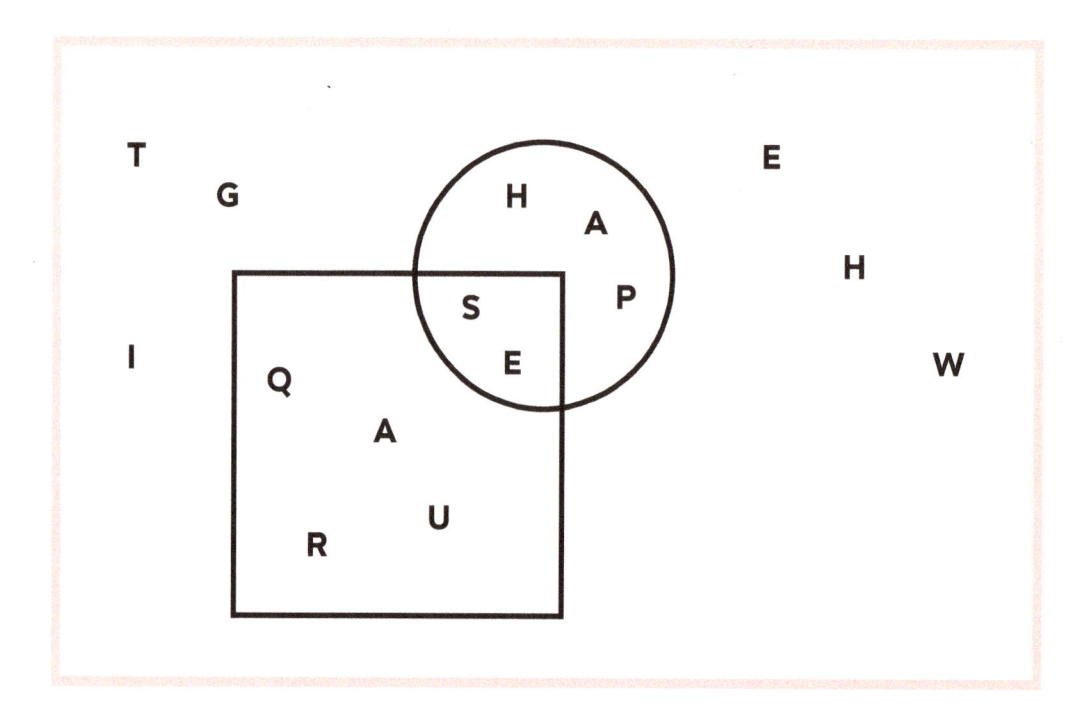

1. What spelling word can you make from the letters in the circle? _____

2. What spelling word can you make from the letters in the square? _____

3. What spelling word can you make with the letters you haven't used yet? _____

Words to Learn: MORE MEASUREMENT AND MATH WORDS

Write each word in the blank.

1. number _____
2. digit _____
3. even _____
4. odd _____
5. half _____
6. whole _____
7. multiply _____
8. divide _____
9. addition _____
10. subtraction _____

Write your hardest words again here:

_____

_____

PUZZLE 66

Merry-Go-Round

Start at any letter and move around the circle, either forward or backward, to find one of your spelling words. Circle the first letter of the word you find. Write the word under each circle.

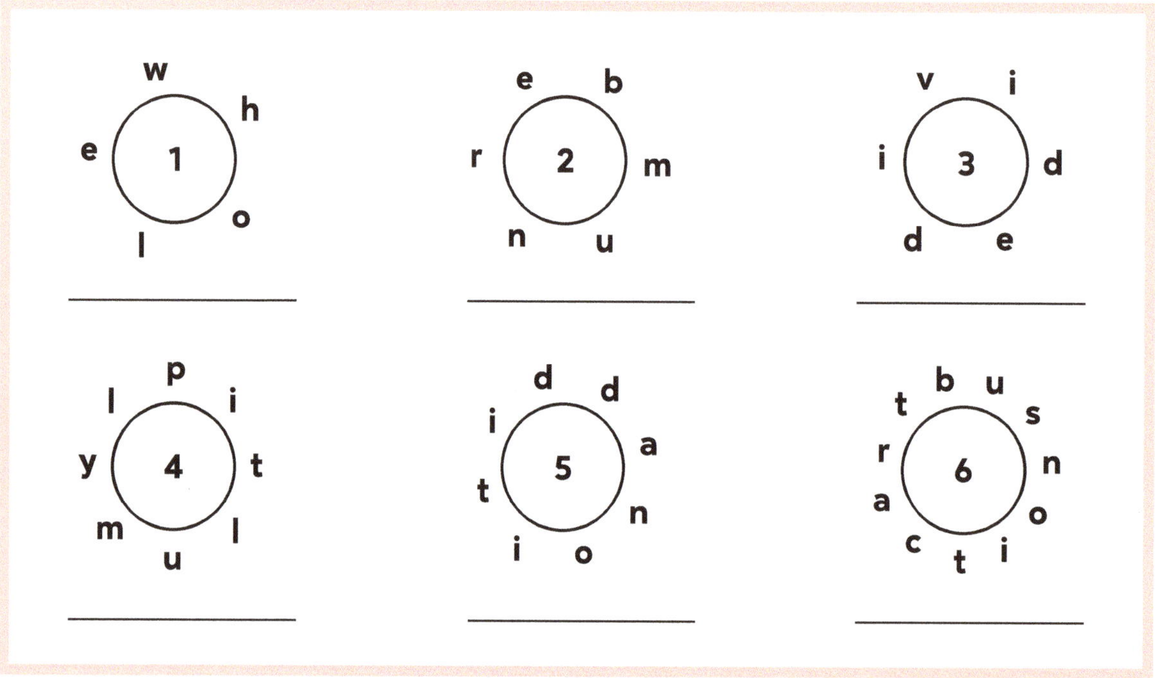
1
w h o l e
2
e b m u n r
3
v i d e d i
4
p i t l u m y l
5
d d a n o i t i
6
b u s n o i t c a r t

Write a sentence using a spelling word of your choice.

PUZZLE 67

Tic-Tac-Toe

Circle every word that is spelled correctly. Draw a line across three of them to score a tic-tac-toe. Write the misspelled words correctly in the blanks.

adition	digitt	even
numer	odd	wole
divide	subtration	multiply

_____

_____

Words to Learn: More Measurement and Math Words

PUZZLE 68

Circle Time

In each line, circle the first, third, fifth, and seventh letters, and so on. Write the circled letters on the first blank. Write the leftover letters on the second blank. You will discover two math words.

1. e o v d e d n

   _____

   _____

2. w h h a o l l f e

   _____

   _____

3. n d u i m g b i e t r

   _____

   _____

4. a m d u d l i t t i i p o l n y

   _____

   _____

Write a sentence using one pair of words listed above.

_____

_____

82   The 3rd Grade Spelling Workbook

PUZZLE 69

Letter Sense

Add the missing letters to your spelling words so each sentence makes sense.

1. We learned how to multiply two- ___ ___ ___ ___t numbers today in math class.

2. What's the largest ___ ___ ___ b ___ ___ you can write?

3. When you ___ ___ ___ ___ ___ e 100 by 2, the answer is 50.

4. When you ___ ___ ___ t ___ ___ ___ ___ 50 by 2, the answer is 100.

5. You can use ___ ___ ___ i ___ ___ ___ n to find the total number of objects.

6. You can use ___ ___ ___ t ___ ___ ___ ___ ___ ___ n to find the difference between two numbers.

PUZZLE 70

Word Search

Circle each word from the list that you find in the word search. Words may go up, down, across, or diagonally, both backward and forward. Write each word as you find it.

M	N	T	V	W	F	Q	Q	Q	D	W
N	O	N	U	M	B	E	R	O	M	H
V	I	I	H	V	E	H	S	D	U	O
J	T	O	N	U	U	A	T	D	L	L
I	C	R	O	A	M	L	J	Q	T	E
W	A	N	I	C	D	F	O	Y	I	O
Y	R	D	T	B	F	I	A	C	P	G
E	T	T	I	B	O	S	V	J	L	M
V	B	J	D	G	H	Q	I	I	Y	U
E	U	Y	D	E	I	Z	D	I	D	J
N	S	J	A	J	G	T	Y	W	K	E

number _____ divide _____

digit _____ half _____

even _____ whole _____

odd _____ addition _____

multiply _____ subtraction _____

84   The 3rd Grade Spelling Workbook

Words to Learn: EARTH WORDS

Write each word in the blank.

1. earth   _____
2. soil   _____
3. lava   _____
4. heat   _____
5. wind   _____
6. frost   _____
7. clouds   _____
8. rainstorm   _____
9. weather   _____
10. seasons   _____

Write your hardest words again here:

_____

_____

PUZZLE 71

Bubbles!

Color in the bubbles you need to spell each word in the box. Unscramble the leftover bubbles to spell another word from the list on page 85. Write that word in the blank.

soil   weather   clouds   seasons   rainstorm

New word: _____

PUZZLE 72

Word Match

Write the letter for each spelling word from the box in front of the correct meaning. Write the spelling word in the blank at the end. If your work is right, you'll spell a fun word in the beginning blanks! Copy that word into the blanks at the bottom.

1. ____ Ice that forms from water vapor _____

2. ____ Objects that form in the sky from millions of water droplets and/or tiny pieces of ice _____

3. ____ Magma at the earth's surface _____

4. ____ Loose top layer of the earth's surface, suitable for growing plants _____

5. ____ Air that moves over the earth _____

N. clouds   W. soil
O. lava   Y. wind
S. frost

Fun word: ___ ___ ___ ___ ___

Words to Learn: Earth Words

PUZZLE 73

Crack the Code

Use the code to find your spelling words. Write each letter as you solve it.

1. 1 4 9 6 ♥

   __ __ __ __ __

2. 3 7 8 5

   __ __ __ __

3. ↑ 9 7 3 6

   __ __ __ __ __

4. ? 5 7 ⇔ ♦ 3

   __ __ __ __ __ __

5. # 1 4 6 ♥ 1 9

   __ __ __ __ __ __ __

6. 3 1 4 3 7 2 3

   __ __ __ __ __ __ __

7. 9 4 8 2 3 6 7 9 $

   __ __ __ __ __ __ __ __ __

1 = E	7 = O	$ = M
2 = N	8 = I	+ = V
3 = S	9 = R	# = W
4 = A	♦ = D	↑ = F
5 = L	♥ = H	? = C
6 = T	⇔ = U	

88   The 3rd Grade Spelling Workbook

PUZZLE 74

Box Stop

Write one word from the box in each blank space. You will not use all of the words.

| clouds | rainstorm | weather | seasons | earth |
| soil | lava | wind | heat | frost |

1. What word describes matter that comes out of a volcano?
   _____

2. What things sometimes happen when there is thunder?
   _____ _____

3. There are four of these in a year.
   _____

4. Heat, cold, rain, wind, and sunshine are all parts of this.
   _____

5. What word, when spelled with a capital letter, names the planet where we live?
   _____

Words to Learn: Earth Words

PUZZLE 75

Crisscross

Choose two earth words from the box for each crisscross puzzle. (Use words that share the same letter.) Write the words in the puzzle. Write the words again on the lines below each puzzle.

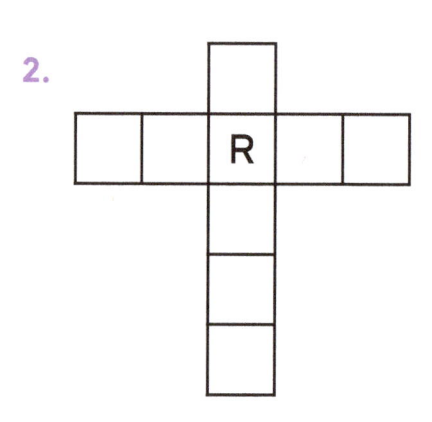

| soil | earth | wind | weather |
| lava | frost | clouds | seasons |

1.

L

_____ _____

2.

R

_____ _____

3.

D

4.

A

_____ _____

Words to Learn: SPACE WORDS

Write each word in the blank.

1. space _____
2. moon _____
3. crater _____
4. orbit _____
5. planet _____
6. comet _____
7. Milky Way _____
8. rocket _____
9. telescope _____
10. astronaut _____

Write your hardest words again here:

_____

_____

PUZZLE 76

ABC Order

Circle the first letter of each word in the box. Write all eight words in ABC order in the blanks.

| space | moon | crater | orbit |
| planet | rocket | telescope | astronaut |

1. _____
2. _____
3. _____
4. _____
5. _____
6. _____
7. _____
8. _____

Write a sentence using the first word on your list.

_____

_____

PUZZLE 77

Merry-Go-Round

Start at any letter and move around the circle, either forward or backward, to find one of your spelling words. Circle the first letter of the word you find. Write the word under each circle.

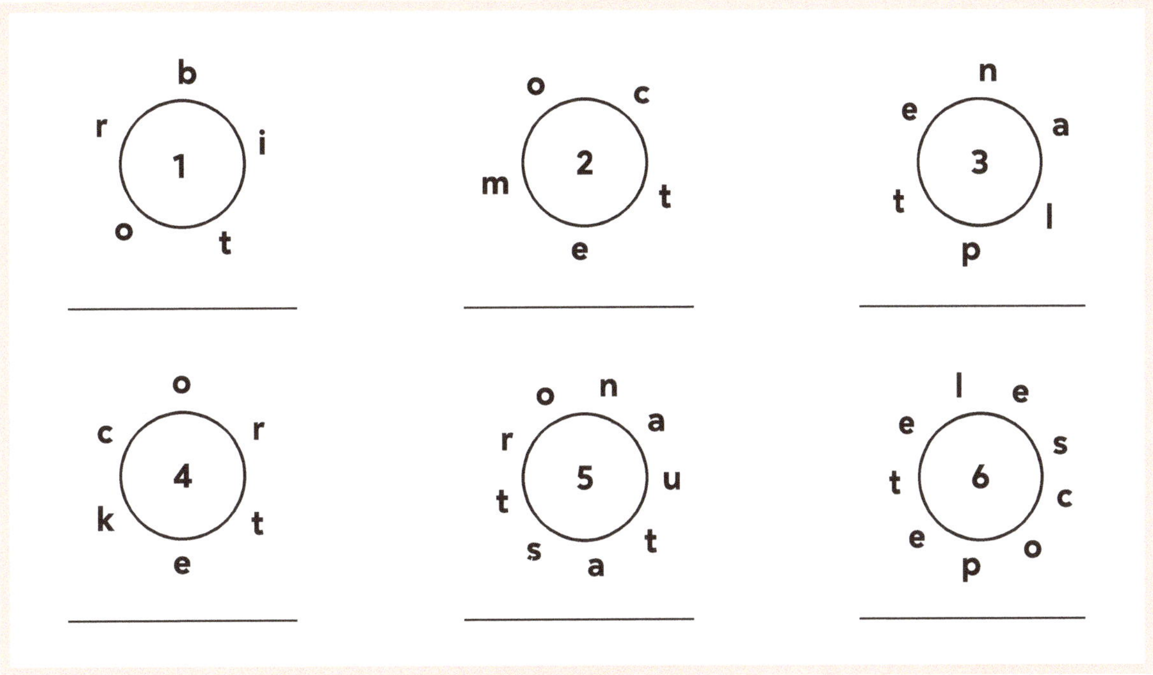

1
b i t o r
2
o c t e m
3
n a l p t e
4
o r t e k c
5
o n a u t a s t r
6
l e s c o p e t e

PUZZLE 78

Letter Sense

Add the missing letters to your spelling words so each sentence makes sense.

1. We live in the M ___ ___ ___ ___ W ___ ___ galaxy.

2. The name of our ___ ___ a n ___ ___ is Earth.

3. There is one ___ ___ ___ n that is in ___ ___ ___ ___ t around our planet.

4. How would you like to travel in outer ___ ___ ___ c ___?

5. Would you like to become an a___ t r ___ ___ ___ ___ t?

6. A spacecraft is often launched by a ___ ___ c k ___ ___.

7. You can use a ___ ___ l e ___ c ___ p ___ to look at faraway stars.

PUZZLE 79

Be Choosy!

Choose the best answer to complete the sentence and circle it. Write the word in the blank.

1. It takes the moon about one month to _____ the Earth.

    orbit   comet   rocket

2. A dip in the moon's surface is called a _____.

    planet   crater   comet

3. As a _____ gets close to the sun, it gets a long tail.

    planet   moon   comet

4. Let's look through the _____ and try to find Mars.

    rocket   telescope   crater

5. There is no gravity in _____.

    space   rocket   comet

6. That is why an _____ floats inside the spacecraft.

    telescope   moon   astronaut

PUZZLE 80

Tic-Tac-Toe

Circle every word that is spelled correctly. Draw a line across three of them to score a tic-tac-toe. Write the misspelled words correctly in the blanks.

crator	comet	planit
orbat	rocket	astronat
telscope	moon	Milky Way

_____

_____

Words to Learn: EVERYDAY WORDS

Write each word in the blank.

1. Sunday _____
2. Monday _____
3. Tuesday _____
4. Wednesday _____
5. Thursday _____
6. Friday _____
7. Saturday _____
8. week _____
9. month _____
10. year _____

Write your hardest words again here:

_____

_____

PUZZLE 81

Bubbles!

Color in the bubbles you need to spell each word in the box. Unscramble the leftover bubbles to spell another word from the list on page 97. Write that word in the blank.

| Sunday | Tuesday | Friday | Saturday | year |

New word: _____

98   The 3rd Grade Spelling Workbook

PUZZLE 82

Word Search

Circle each word from the list that you find in the word search. Words may go up, down, across, or diagonally, both backward and forward. Write each word as you find it.

D	J	M	Y	E	A	R	S	H	Y
Y	K	Y	A	D	N	U	S	P	Y
Y	W	W	C	W	G	M	T	F	A
A	N	E	C	B	T	O	J	C	D
D	K	S	D	G	J	N	T	O	N
R	E	W	L	N	C	T	L	G	O
U	E	J	R	F	E	H	N	R	M
T	W	Y	O	S	D	S	V	V	F
A	Y	A	D	I	R	F	D	H	K
S	A	T	H	U	R	S	D	A	Y
N	M	Y	A	D	S	E	U	T	Y

Sunday _____ Friday _____

Monday _____ Saturday _____

Tuesday _____ week _____

Wednesday _____ month _____

Thursday _____ year _____

Words to Learn: Everyday Words

PUZZLE 83

Shape Shake-Up

Look closely at the letters in the shapes. Answer the questions below.

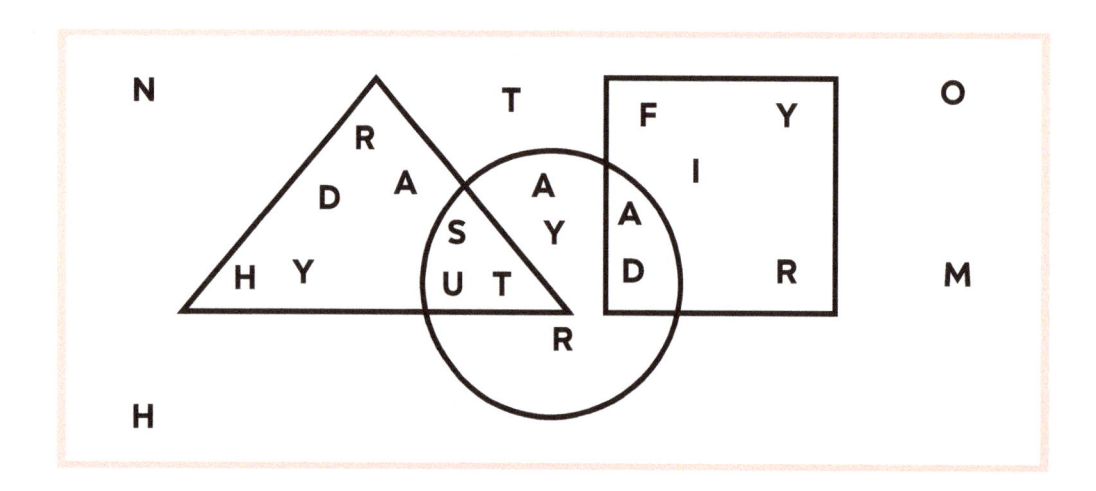

```
N          T         F    Y        O
     R          A
  D        S  Y    A
 H   Y      U T    D    R         M
                R
H
```

1. What spelling word can you make from the letters in the circle? _____

2. What spelling word can you make from the letters in the square? _____

3. What spelling word can you make from the letters in the triangle? _____

4. What spelling word can you make with the letters you haven't used yet? _____

PUZZLE 84

Box Stop

Write one word from the box in each blank space. You will not use all of the words.

| Sunday | Monday | Tuesday | Wednesday | Thursday |
| Friday | Saturday | week | month | year |

1. On most calendars, the first day of the week is _____.

2. The day after Monday is _____.

3. The day before Friday is _____.

4. The middle day of the week is _____.

5. There are 52 weeks in one _____.

6. Each _____ has between 28 and 31 days.

Words to Learn: Everyday Words

PUZZLE 85

Crisscross

Choose two everyday words from the box for each crisscross puzzle. (Use words that share the same letter.) Write the words in the puzzle. Write the words again on the lines below each puzzle.

| week | Monday | Tuesday | Thursday |
| Friday | year | Saturday | Sunday |

1. E

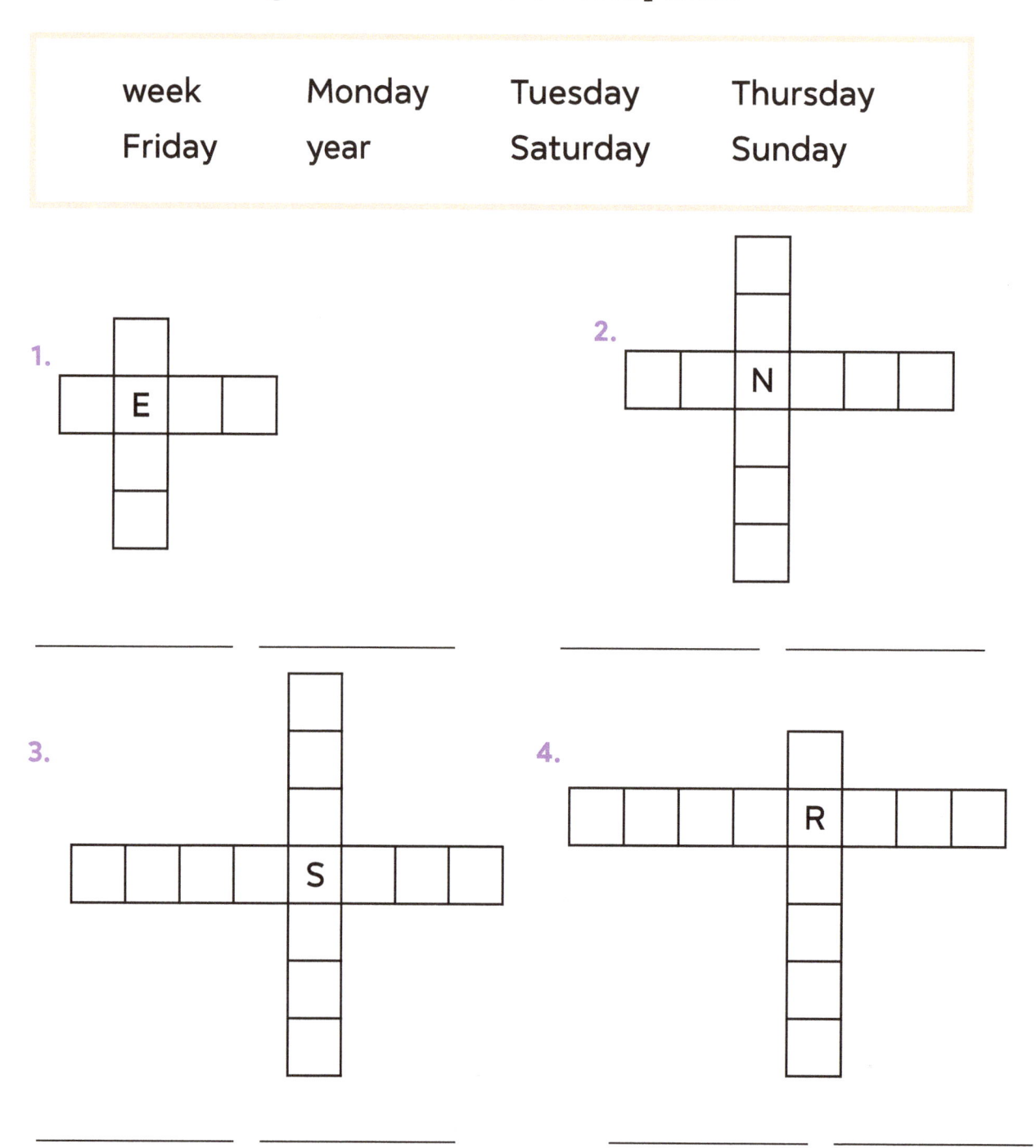

2. N

3. S

4. R

_____ _____

_____ _____

102   The 3rd Grade Spelling Workbook

Words to Learn: MORE EVERYDAY WORDS

Write each word in the blank.

1. breakfast _____
2. lunch _____
3. dinner _____
4. already _____
5. doesn't _____
6. believe _____
7. answer _____
8. until _____
9. although _____
10. enough _____

Write your hardest words again here:

_____

_____

PUZZLE 86

Merry-Go-Round

Start at any letter and move around the circle, either forward or backward, to find one of your spelling words. Circle the first letter of the word you find. Write the word under each circle.

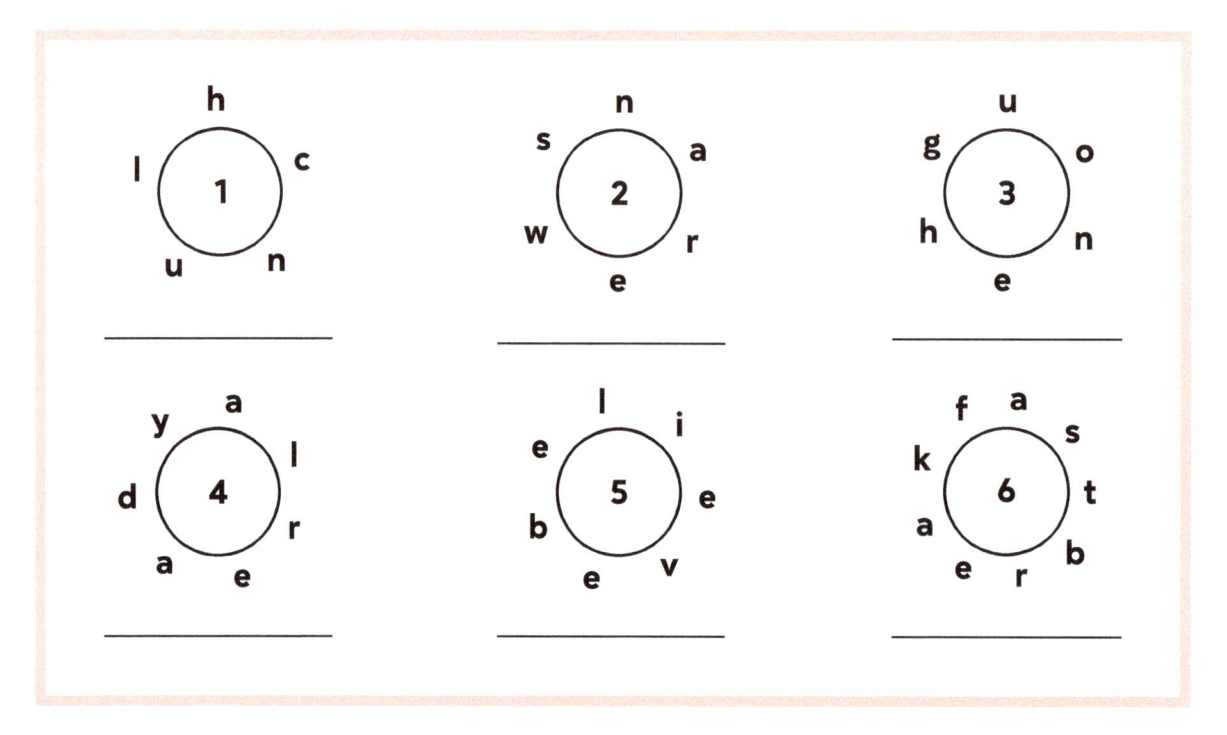

1. h, c, n, u, l — lunch
2. n, a, r, e, w, s — answer
3. u, o, n, e, h, g — enough
4. a, l, r, e, a, d, y — already
5. l, i, e, v, e, b — believe
6. a, s, t, b, r, e, a, k, f — breakfast

Write a sentence using the hardest word to spell above.

_____

_____

_____

_____

PUZZLE 87

Tic-Tac-Toe

Circle every word that is spelled correctly. Draw a line across three of them to score a tic-tac-toe. Write the misspelled words correctly in the blanks.

anser	dosen't	although
untill	breakfast	dinner
lunch	enough	beleive

_____

_____

Words to Learn: More Everyday Words   105

PUZZLE 88

Be Choosy!

Choose the best answer to complete the sentence and circle it. Write the word in the blank.

1. It's best to start your day with a good _____.

    breakfast   enough   already

2. Do you know the _____ to this question?

    until   although   answer

3. Please do not give me any more food because I have enough _____.

    doesn't   already   believe

4. I _____ my parents always tell me the truth.

    believe   until   lunch

5. My friend _____ have as many toys as I do, so I share mine with her.

    although   doesn't   answer

6. Please don't start the party _____ we get there.

    until   doesn't   already

PUZZLE 89

Finish the Poem

Finish this rhyming poem. Use one of the spelling words from the box in each blank. (There is one extra word.) If time allows, draw a picture to go with your poem on another piece of paper.

| believe | until | already | enough | lunch | dinner |

Dad is the winner

When it comes to __ __ __ __ __ __.

My friends can't __ __ __ __ __ __ __

What he has up his sleeve!

He makes carrots, roasts, and lemon fluff.

You can eat and eat until you've had __ __ __ __ __ __.

He says if I can keep my hands nice and steady,

He'll teach me to make cream puffs __ __ __ __ __ __ __.

Dad likes to cook dinner, but in a crunch,

He says that I can make a very good __ __ __ __ __!

Words to Learn: More Everyday Words

PUZZLE 90

Word Search Challenge

Circle each word from the list that you find in the word search. Words may go up, down, across, or diagonally, both backward and forward. Write each word as you find it. Please note: There is no apostrophe in the puzzle.

Challenge: Two of the words appear twice. Can you find them? Circle those words in your word list.

H	R	H	T	R	B	B	H	A	I	H	A
C	V	E	S	U	N	T	I	L	V	B	A
N	N	U	N	L	O	U	L	T	G	E	T
U	T	H	E	N	O	U	G	H	I	N	O
L	U	S	B	Y	I	V	W	O	A	O	A
R	E	U	A	B	D	D	E	U	N	U	N
H	E	V	B	F	E	A	V	G	L	G	S
B	O	V	E	B	K	L	E	H	N	H	W
U	R	V	I	I	L	A	I	R	G	I	E
G	U	A	V	O	L	A	E	E	L	S	R
V	E	H	A	B	U	E	E	R	V	A	V
O	D	O	E	S	N	T	B	B	B	E	V

breakfast _____   believe _____

lunch _____   answer _____

dinner _____   until _____

already _____   although _____

doesn't _____   enough _____

108   The 3rd Grade Spelling Workbook

PUZZLE 91

ABC Order

You learned 180 words in this book, from A to Z! Now can you put 14 of those words in ABC order? Circle the first letter of each word in the box. Write all the words in ABC order in the blanks.

lava	globe	prism	zoo	noise
airport	message	whole	baseball	shopping
eagle	city	year	hamster	

1. _____
2. _____
3. _____
4. _____
5. _____
6. _____
7. _____
8. _____
9. _____
10. _____
11. _____
12. _____
13. _____
14. _____

Words to Learn: More Everyday Words

Extra Practice

PUZZLE 92

Letter Sense: ER and OR Words

Add the missing letters to your spelling words so each sentence makes sense. Two of the missing letters in each word will be ER or OR.

1. Friends are coming to our house for ___ i n n ___ ___.

2. After we eat, we will watch boats come in to the ___ ___ r b ___ ___.

3. Which c o l ___ ___ of boat do you like best?

4. Be sure to drink lots of water when you travel to the d e s ___ ___ t.

5. When we cross the b ___ ___ d e r, we want to buy some p o t ___ ___ ___ y.

6. We want to go to the ___ a k ___ ___ y for fresh bread.

7. We can also use the i n t ___ ___ n e t there and check our email.

8. Hopefully, I'll remember my p a ___ ___ w ___ ___ d.

9. The w e a t h ___ ___ will change when we drive n ___ ___ t ___.

10. Someday, I want to travel around the entire w ___ ___ ___ d!

Extra Practice

PUZZLE 93

Odd One Out: Letter Sounds

Each line has four words. But one word does not belong. Sometimes the same letters make different sounds. Or, sometimes the same sounds are made by different letters.

Circle the word in each line that does not belong. In the blank, tell why the word does not belong.

1. gulf   chalk   golf   wolf

_____

2. heat   weave   seasons   earth

_____

3. circle   hospital   fiddle   turtle

_____

4. fuzzy   valley   hockey   monkey

_____

5. tuba   brush   skunk   subway

_____

6. lunch   archery   catch   school

_____

7. throw   although   arrow   rainbow

_____

Extra Practice

PUZZLE 94

Silly Story: Word Endings and Days of the Week

Circle all the misspelled words in this silly story. You may find misspelled words from any chapter in this book. Write all the misspelled words correctly on the lines on the next page.

AN EXCITING DAY

"Hooray! Today is Thersday! Let's all go swimming," cried Louis.

"No, this is Wednsday," said Rosa. "This is the day we go bowlling."

"I am sorry to tell you," chuckled Mom, "but you are both mistaken. This is Teusday, and we are going shoping."

"Not shopping," said both kids with a sigh. "Can't we please do something else?"

Just then, Mom's cell phone rang. Mom slipped into the other room and spoke in a quiet voice.

Soon she was walking back into the room with a big smile on her face. "Your Aunt Amy has just offered to make a fun additoin to our day, but only if you want to go with her."

"Anything is better than shoping," mumbled Louis.

"Aunt Amy always has fun ideas," said Rosa. "I vote *YES!*"

"Dosen't anyone want to hear Aunt Amy's idea first?" Mom asked.

"Yes, yes, of course we do!" both children answered together.

"Aunt Amy wants to take you to the circus," Mom replied with a twinkle in her eye. "Now, who wants to go shopping, and who wants to go to the circus?"

Mom did not even wait for their ansers before she dialed Aunt Amy's number to say *YES* to the circus.

Extra Practice

PUZZLE 95

Shape Shake-Up: Words That End with Vowels

Look closely at the letters in the shapes. Answer the questions below.

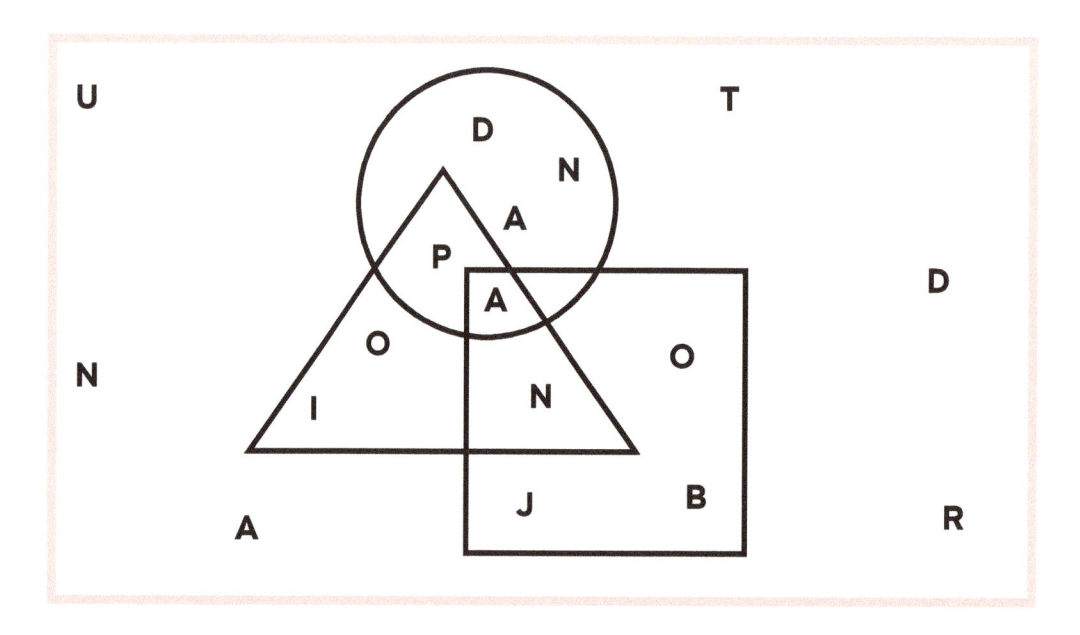

```
U                          T
        D
          N
        A
      P
        A              D
      O       O
N   I       N
        J    B
A                        R
```

1. What spelling word can you make from the letters in the circle? _____

2. What spelling word can you make from the letters in the triangle? _____

3. What spelling word can you make from the letters in the square? _____

4. What spelling word can you make with the letters you haven't used yet? _____

Extra Practice

PUZZLE 96

Word Search: Three-Syllable Words

In this book, you learned some big words! Do you remember how to spell them? First, add the missing letters to each of these words. Then find the completed words in the puzzle and circle them. The words may appear in any direction in the puzzle.

S __ t __ rd __ y   M ___ k y W __ y   s __ b t r __ c t ___ n

c __ m p __ t __ r   m __ n __ r __ l   ap __ r __ m __ nt

oct __ p __ s   s __ x __ ph __ ne   astr __ n ___ t

c __ nt __ n __ nt   tel __ sc __ p __   gr __ ssh __ pp __ r

S	O	H	T	E	L	E	S	C	O	P	E	N
G	U	G	S	E	N	O	H	P	O	X	A	S
A	T	B	R	L	M	I	L	K	Y	W	A	Y
R	N	G	T	A	S	T	R	O	N	A	U	T
E	E	O	L	R	S	P	E	H	P	V	I	V
T	M	C	V	E	A	S	O	G	H	F	S	E
U	T	T	Z	N	S	C	H	I	Y	Z	Z	H
P	R	O	N	I	R	G	T	O	T	M	R	Q
M	A	P	G	M	N	W	O	I	P	J	L	K
O	P	U	D	W	W	P	H	W	O	P	S	U
C	A	S	Z	Y	N	T	N	F	D	N	E	S
Y	C	O	N	T	I	N	E	N	T	B	Z	R
S	A	T	U	R	D	A	Y	A	Q	G	K	E

Extra Practice   **115**

Extra Practice

PUZZLE 97

Hidden Message: Multiple-Meaning Words

Some of the spelling words you learned in this book have more than one meaning. Think about the word *foot,* for example. It can mean "the part of your body at the end of your leg." It can also mean "12 inches."

In this activity you will find two clues for the same word. Choose one spelling word from the box that has both of those meanings. Write it in the blanks. Copy the numbered letters into the blanks at the bottom of page 117 that have the same numbers.

You will spell the answer to this joke: *Why should you wear boots when it's raining cats and dogs?*

| tablet | wind | cape | picture |
| matter | frost | odd | light |

1. A point of land that extends out into the water AND

    A piece of clothing that hangs over the shoulders

    and back __ __ __ __
                 4

2. A covering of tiny ice crystals AND

    To put icing on a cake or cookies __ __ __ __ __
                                    9 1

3. A design made by drawing or painting AND

   An idea in your mind __ __ __ __ __ __ __
                                           8   2   3

4. Energy from the sun that makes it possible to see AND

   Not heavy __ __ __ __ __
                5

5. Anything that takes up space and has mass AND

   A topic of interest or concern __ __ __ __ __ __
                                7   13

6. A movement of air AND

   Breath, as in "That climb knocked the _____

   out of me!" __ __ __ __
               6 11

7. Numbers that are not even AND

   Only one of a pair or set __ __ __
                        10

8. A thin, portable computer AND

   A pill or small piece of medicine __ __ __ __ __ __
                                     12

Why should you wear boots when it's raining cats and dogs?

Because you might __ __ __ __ __ __ __
                1 2 3 4 5 6 7

__ __ __ __ __ __!
8 9 10 11 12 13

Extra Practice

ANSWER KEY

PUZZLE 1

New word: PANDA

PUZZLE 2

1. bear
2. hamster
3. lamb
4. mouse
5. panda
6. skunk
7. wolf
8. zebra

Sentences will vary.

PUZZLE 3

1. snail, turtle
2. zebra, panda, skunk
3. lamb
4. Answers will vary.

Sentences will vary.

PUZZLE 4

V	T	U	R	T	L	E	S	S
R	E	T	S	M	A	H	I	N
P	S	S	Z	R	J	Y	C	X
W	L	N	E	W	Y	C	M	K
S	O	A	B	M	N	N	T	M
K	L	I	R	M	O	U	S	E
U	A	L	A	D	N	A	P	D
N	M	Y	E	X	F	Q	B	K
K	B	W	B	N	F	L	O	W

PUZZLE 5

skunk, snail, lamb, bear, panda

PUZZLE 6

1. monkey
2. eagle
3. spider
4. giraffe
5. octopus
6. goldfish

PUZZLE 7

1. octopus
2. grasshopper
3. jellyfish
4. spider
5. turkey
6. robin
7. goldfish

PUZZLE 8

1. monkey
2. giraffe
3. robin
4. eagle
5. turkey
6. goldfish

PUZZLE 9

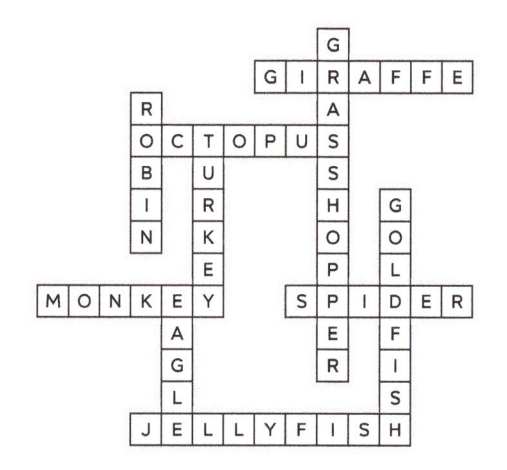

(crossword with: GIRAFFE, OCTOPUS, MONKEY, SPIDER, JELLYFISH, ROBIN, BUNK/BUNKER, GRASSHOPPER, GOLDFISH)

PUZZLE 10

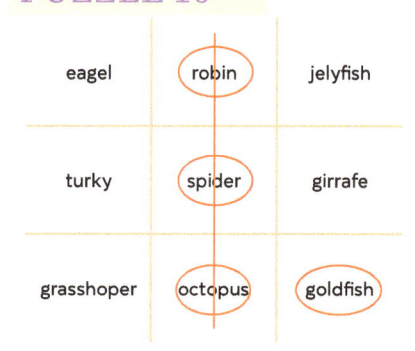

eagel	robin	jelyfish
turky	spider	girrafe
grasshoper	octopus	goldfish

(circled: robin, spider, octopus, goldfish)

Corrections: eagle, jellyfish, turkey, giraffe, grasshopper

PUZZLE 11

1. S, running
2. P, coach
3. O, player
4. R, swimming
5. T, teammates

Fun word: SPORT

Sentences will vary.

118

PUZZLE 12

S	A	M	I	P	L	A	Y	E	R
W	W	E	T	S	R	R	O	R	L
G	N	I	L	W	O	B	A	E	L
A	R	F	M	C	A	T	C	H	A
S	E	T	A	M	M	A	E	T	B
J	O	H	Z	D	I	D	L	Z	T
T	E	G	N	I	N	N	U	R	O
C	O	A	C	H	E	M	G	K	O
T	H	R	O	W	A	R	U	R	F
O	L	L	A	B	E	S	A	B	K

PUZZLE 13

1. teammates
2. coach
3. bowling
4. swimming
5. baseball
6. throw

PUZZLE 14

1. coach
2. running
3. catch
4. swimming
5. player
6. football
7. teammates

PUZZLE 15

1. catch/coach
2. football/throw
3. swimming/running
4. teammates/player

PUZZLE 16

1. archery
2. biking
3. golf
4. hockey
5. mascot
6. racing
7. soccer

Sentences will vary.

PUZZLE 17

1. skating
2. helmet
3. arrow
4. hockey
5. biking
6. mascot

PUZZLE 18

1. skating, racing, biking
2. helmet
3. arrow
4. hockey
5. soccer

Sentences will vary.

PUZZLE 19

1. biking/helmet
2. archery/racing
3. soccer/hockey
4. skating/mascot

Sentences will vary.

PUZZLE 20

1. golf
2. mascot
3. skating, skating
4. archery
5. soccer
6. biking
7. helmet

PUZZLE 21

New word: CHALK

PUZZLE 22

coler	(weave)	potery
(print)	(brush)	(drawing)
cartune	crayen	picher

Corrections: color, pottery, cartoon, crayon, picture

PUZZLE 23

1. color
2. picture
3. pottery
4. chalk
5. weave
6. brush

PUZZLE 24

C	Q	T	Y	R	E	T	T	O	P
C	J	N	O	Y	A	R	C	P	I
A	N	P	E	V	A	E	W	R	M
R	B	W	I	N	E	N	M	I	J
T	V	R	T	C	D	Z	H	N	J
O	K	O	U	V	T	G	T	T	E
O	L	L	G	S	A	U	M	J	H
N	A	O	K	E	H	U	R	D	L
S	H	C	K	D	J	G	M	E	U
P	C	S	D	R	A	W	I	N	G

PUZZLE 25

1. color/chalk
2. crayon/brush
3. drawing/weave
4. picture/cartoon

PUZZLE 26

1. flute
2. banjo
3. fiddle
4. bagpipes
5. trumpet
6. saxophone

Sentences will vary.

PUZZLE 27

1. tuba
2. piano
3. drums
4. trumpet
5. fiddle
6. trombone
7. saxophone

Sentences will vary.

PUZZLE 28

PUZZLE 29

1. flute, bagpipes, trumpet, saxophone, tuba, trombone
2. trombone
3. drums, fiddle
4. piano, banjo, fiddle

Sentences will vary.

PUZZLE 30

1. flute
2. drums
3. trumpet
4. piano
5. fiddle
6. trombone
7. saxophone

PUZZLE 31

1. coast
2. east
3. gulf
4. mountain
5. north
6. river
7. south
8. valley
9. west

Sentences will vary.

PUZZLE 32

New word: STREAM

PUZZLE 33

PUZZLE 34

1. river
2. west
3. gulf
4. coast
5. mountain
6. valley

PUZZLE 35

1. east/west
2. north/south
3. stream/river
4. valley/coast

PUZZLE 36

1. world
2. globe
3. desert
4. glacier
5. tundra
6. harbor

PUZZLE 37

1. globe
2. border
3. glacier
4. cape
5. tundra

PUZZLE 38

1. globe/world
2. nation/border
3. glacier/tundra
4. harbor/desert

Sentences will vary.

120 Answer Key

PUZZLE 39

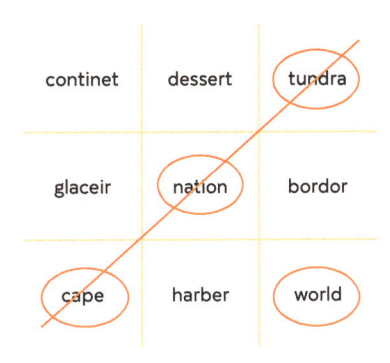

continet	dessert	tundra
glaceir	nation	bordor
cape	harber	world

Corrections: continent, desert, glacier, border, harbor

PUZZLE 40

1. border
2. harbor
3. desert
4. nation
5. glacier
6. continent

PUZZLE 41

New word: SCHOOL

PUZZLE 42

1. airport
2. bakery
3. city
4. noise
5. bookstore
6. people

PUZZLE 43

```
T A I R P O R T W S
D K I C S C B V Z S
M L C I T Y O I T C
P A K P C S O E H H
K W R P W A K L C O
H E Q K N K S P R O
J D J Z E R T O U L
N I L J M T O E H S
E S I O N U R P C C
O N W L Y R E K A B
```

PUZZLE 44

1. P, city
2. A, market
3. R, school
4. K, church
5. S, airport

Fun word: PARKS

PUZZLE 45

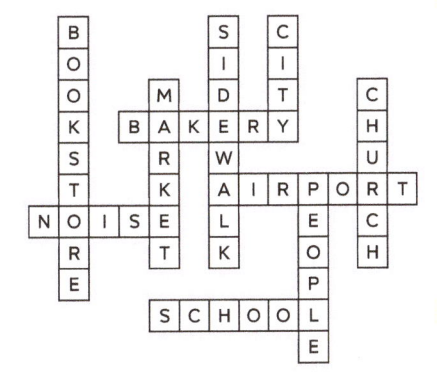

Crossword with answers: BOOKSTORE, MARKET, NOISE, SIDEWALK, CITY, BAKERY, AIRPORT, CHURCH, PEOPLE, SCHOOL

PUZZLE 46

1. circus
2. hospital
3. walking
4. subway
5. shopping
6. offices

PUZZLE 47

taxie	apartment	sircus
shoping	walkking	hosptal
street	offices	subway

Corrections: taxi, circus, shopping, walking, hospital

PUZZLE 48

1. taxi, subway, walking
2. hospital
3. apartment
4. zoo, circus

Sentences will vary.

PUZZLE 49

1. taxi/zoo
2. subway/street
3. walking/offices
4. apartment/hospital

Sentences will vary.

PUZZLE 50

1. taxi
2. circus
3. walking
4. apartments
5. offices
6. street
7. zoo

Answer Key 121

PUZZLE 51

New word: ENERGY
Sentences will vary.

PUZZLE 52

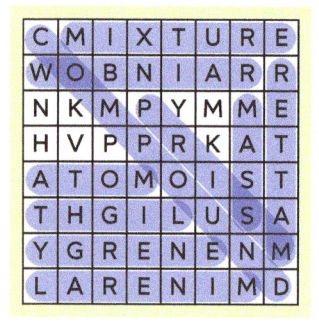

```
C M I X T U R E
W O B N I A R R
N K M P Y M M E
H V P P R K A T
A T O M O I S T
T H G I L U S A
Y G R E N E N M
L A R E N I M D
```

Sentences will vary.

PUZZLE 53

1. atom
2. mass
3. matter
4. light
5. mineral
6. rainbow
7. prism
8. compound

Sentences will vary.

PUZZLE 54

1. atom/mass
2. rainbow/prism
3. mixture/mineral
4. matter/energy

PUZZLE 55

1. prism
2. rainbow
3. mixture
4. atom
5. energy
6. mass

PUZZLE 56

1. tablet
2. screen
3. password
4. robot
5. message
6. computer

Sentences will vary.

PUZZLE 57

1. G, internet
2. A, tablet
3. M, password
4. E, screen
5. S, message

Fun word: GAMES

PUZZLE 58

1. robot
2. camera
3. tablet
4. device
5. computer
6. screen
7. internet

PUZZLE 59

1. camera/robot
2. tablet/device
3. computer/password
4. cell phone/internet

Sentences will vary.

PUZZLE 60

1. MESSAGE
2. CAMERA
3. COMPUTER

PUZZLE 61

1. circle
2. foot
3. inch
4. mile
5. ounce
6. pound
7. square
8. weight
9. yard

Sentences will vary.

PUZZLE 62

New word: INCH
Sentences will vary.

PUZZLE 63

1. inch, foot, yard, mile
2. pound
3. weight
4. shape
5. circle, square

Sentences will vary.

PUZZLE 64

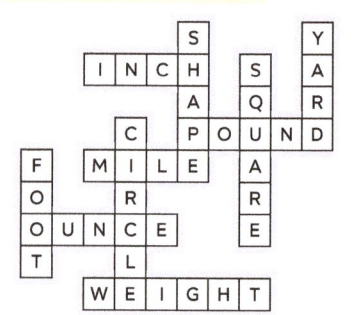

```
        S           Y
  I N C H   S       A
        A   Q       R
        C   P O U N D
F   M I L E         
O   R               A
O   R               R
U N C E             E
T   L               
    W E I G H T     
```

PUZZLE 65

1. SHAPE
2. SQUARE
3. WEIGHT

Answer Key

PUZZLE 66

1. whole
2. number
3. divide
4. multiply
5. addition
6. subtraction

Sentences will vary.

PUZZLE 67

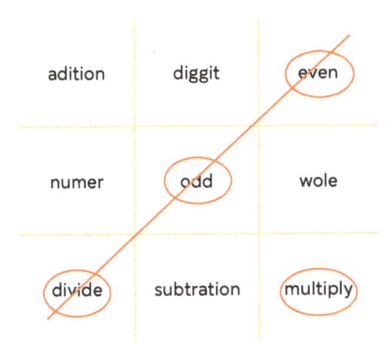

adition	diggit	**even**
numer	**odd**	wole
divide	subtration	**multiply**

Corrections: addition, digit, number, whole, subtraction

PUZZLE 68

1. even/odd
2. whole/half
3. number/digit
4. addition/multiply

Sentences will vary.

PUZZLE 69

1. digit
2. number
3. divide
4. multiply
5. addition
6. subtraction

PUZZLE 70

```
M N T V W F Q Q D W
N O N U M B E R O M H
V I I H V E H S D U O
J T O N U U A T D L L
I C R O A M L J Q T E
W A N I C D F O Y I O
Y R D T B F I A C P G
E T T I B O S V J L M
V B J D G H Q I I Y U
E U Y D E I Z D I D J
N S J A J G T Y W K E
```

PUZZLE 71

New word: LAVA

PUZZLE 72

1. S, frost
2. N, clouds
3. O, lava
4. W, soil
5. Y, wind

Fun word: SNOWY

PUZZLE 73

1. earth
2. soil
3. frost
4. clouds
5. weather
6. seasons
7. rainstorm

PUZZLE 74

1. lava
2. rainstorm, wind
   (Answers may vary.)
3. seasons
4. weather
5. Earth

PUZZLE 75

1. lava/soil
2. earth/frost
3. clouds/wind
4. weather/seasons

PUZZLE 76

1. astronaut
2. crater
3. moon
4. orbit
5. planet
6. rocket
7. space
8. telescope

Sentences will vary.

PUZZLE 77

1. orbit
2. comet
3. planet
4. rocket
5. astronaut
6. telescope

PUZZLE 78

1. Milky Way
2. planet
3. moon, orbit
4. space
5. astronaut
6. rocket
7. telescope

PUZZLE 79

1. orbit
2. crater
3. comet
4. telescope
5. space
6. astronaut

PUZZLE 80

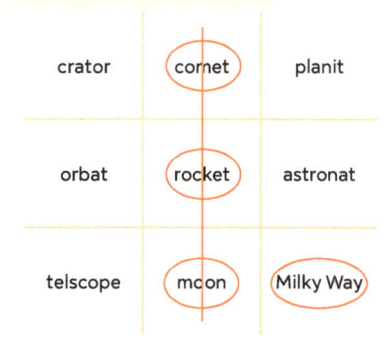

crator	(comet)	planit
orbat	(rocket)	astronat
telscope	(moon)	(Milky Way)

Corrections: crater, planet, orbit, astronaut, telescope

PUZZLE 81

New word: WEEK

PUZZLE 82

(word search grid with YEARS, SUNDAY, THURSDAY, etc.)

PUZZLE 83

1. Saturday
2. Friday
3. Thursday
4. month

PUZZLE 84

1. Sunday
2. Tuesday
3. Thursday
4. Wednesday
5. year
6. month

PUZZLE 85

1. year/week
2. Sunday/Monday
3. Thursday/Tuesday
4. Saturday/Friday

PUZZLE 86

1. lunch
2. answer
3. enough
4. already
5. believe
6. breakfast

Sentences will vary.

PUZZLE 87

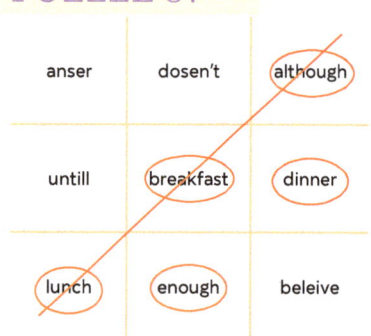

anser	dosen't	(although)
untill	(breakfast)	(dinner)
(lunch)	(enough)	beleive

Corrections: answer, doesn't, until, believe

PUZZLE 88

1. breakfast
2. answer
3. already
4. believe
5. doesn't
6. until

PUZZLE 89

dinner, believe, enough, already, lunch

PUZZLE 90

(word search grid)

The words ENOUGH and BELIEVE appear two times.

PUZZLE 91

1. airport
2. baseball
3. city
4. eagle
5. globe
6. hamster
7. lava
8. message
9. noise
10. prism
11. shopping
12. whole
13. year
14. zoo

124 Answer Key

PUZZLE 92

1. dinner
2. harbor
3. color
4. desert
5. border, pottery
6. bakery
7. internet
8. password
9. weather, north
10. world

PUZZLE 93

These are the words that should be circled, with a brief explanation of why. Reasons may vary slightly.

1. chalk; The L is silent in this word.
2. earth; The EA does not make a long *e* sound in this word.
3. hospital; The final sound is spelled with AL, not LE.
4. fuzzy; The final sound is spelled with Y, not EY.
5. tuba; The U makes a short sound in all the other words.
6. school; Only in this word does the CH make the *k* sound.
7. although; The long *o* sound at the end of the word is not spelled with OW.

PUZZLE 94

Corrected words, in order: Thursday, swimming, Wednesday, bowling, Tuesday, shopping, addition, shopping, doesn't, answers

PUZZLE 95

1. panda
2. piano
3. banjo
4. tundra

PUZZLE 96

Saturday
Milky Way
subtraction
computer
mineral
apartment
octopus
saxophone
astronaut
continent
telescope
grasshopper

PUZZLE 97

1. cape
2. frost
3. picture
4. light
5. matter
6. wind
7. odd
8. tablet

Joke answer: Because you might STEP IN A POODLE!

Answer Key **125**

ACKNOWLEDGMENTS

I wish to thank my husband, Keith, for his support during this fast-paced writing project. In addition to helping with errands, dishes, and laundry, he provided some brilliant ideas when I needed them most.

I am grateful to my friend Jan, who whisked me away to her cottage before the real writing began. We discussed third grade spelling words, but we also shopped, played board games, and laughed a lot!

I appreciate these software creators who offer their helpful programs at no charge:

EclipseCrossword puzzle engine © 1999–2019 Green Eclipse, available at EclipseCrossword.com.

WordSearchCreator V1.0 © 2006–2019 Matthew Wellings.

Finally, I am again indebted to the publishers of these favorite dictionaries from my bookshelf:

de Mello Vianna, Fernando, ed. *Children's Dictionary.* Boston: Houghton Mifflin, 1979.

Abate, Frank, ed. *Oxford Desktop Dictionary and Thesaurus, American Edition.* New York: Berkley Books, 1997.

ABOUT THE AUTHOR

ANN RICHMOND FISHER is the author of *The 2nd Grade Spelling Workbook.* She has also written over 60 books and educational products for a dozen different publishers.

Ann is a former classroom teacher. Now she's known as "Granny Annie" to two children.

Ann has a degree in elementary education from Northern Michigan University. She and her husband, Keith, have lived in Michigan, Indiana, Ireland, and Pennsylvania. They now reside in Ohio.

For more spelling fun, you can visit Ann at one of her two websites: Spelling-Words-Well.com and Word-Game-World.com.